# A Door to All My Rooms

## PEGGY GRAYSON

**ISIS**
LARGE PRINT
Oxford

First published in Great Britain 2000
by Prunus

Published in Large Print 2004 by ISIS Publishing Ltd,
7 Centremead, Osney Mead, Oxford OX2 0ES
by arrangement with Peggy Grayson

**British Library Cataloguing in Publication Data**
Grayson, Peggy
    A door to all my rooms.  – Large print ed.
    – (Isis reminiscence series)
    1. Grayson, Peggy – Childhood and youth
    2. Grayson, Peggy – Homes and haunts –
    England – Berkshire
    3. Large type books
    4. Berkshire (England) – Social life and customs
    5. Berkshire (England) – Biography
    I. Title
    942.2'9083'092

ISBN 0–7531–9944–0 (hb)
ISBN 0–7531–9945–9 (pb)

Printed and bound by Antony Rowe, Chippenham

For Paddy

# CONTENTS

# INTRODUCTION

Foxhill was an old house, set in a small Berkshire village and from 1922 to 1939 was occupied by my mother's parents.

Because my young life had been one of a series of moves from one house to another, Foxhill was "home": warm, safe, unchanging and always welcoming. From my first visit at the age of three, I loved the old house passionately.

I knew and delighted in every room, where each had a place in the scheme of things. In these rooms certain rituals were conducted throughout the year, each at its appointed time.

Memories of those who lived in this little haven, or who came to stay or visit, drift like shades across the span of time. That more gentle existence is now long gone.

Before we too, are shades, and it is too late, I will take you through a door to all my rooms.

# CHAPTER ONE

# Over the Threshold

The door to the house was of hardened oak, painted dark green, furnished with a large, imposing brass knocker in the shape of a lion's head with a ring in its mouth and a capacious letterbox of the same metal, and a large brass door knob too large for my hand when I was a child.

The door was reached by coming through a white wooden gate which squeaked in summer and stuck in winter, off the hard, bright lane where every third year the roadmen came and splashed great sheets of hot tar and topped it with the gold and white gravel from the pits only a few miles away.

The advent of the roadmen, with their cheery, blackened faces and rough jokes, was greeted by the village children with delight, but not more so than the arrival of the huge steam roller with its snorts and puffs of acrid smoke and urgent, clanging bell, as it growled onto the gravel, crushing it into submission with its overpowering weight, and sending tar oozing out to the sides of the road where it stuck to shoes, splashed stockings and trousers and glued the dogs' feet together.

As Foxhill lay in a quiet lane well away from the village, the joy of the village children only became apparent when we went for our walks and heard them cheeking the men and getting chased with a tar brush for their pains.

Between the lane and the front gate was a wide strip of grass, kept close-mown, and as you faced the bland face of the stone built house, a white wooden fence stretched from the right to the back gates where a fifteen foot laurel hedge took over, and on the left to the little one acre meadow girt about with hawthorn hedges.

The front part of the house, which faced north, was further darkened by an enormous Deodar tree, that sprang from the front lawn and towered above the roof, one giant green finger pointing towards the sky.

At the five-barred back gate was an equally large but less imposing "monkey-puzzle" whose lower branches were brown and ragged. I felt I was the only friend to this beleaguered specimen of the genus "Araucaria auracana". Grannie hated it and was all for cutting it down but Gramps, perverse as usual, refused to obey her command, although he was the first to admit it was an eyesore and the brown, shrivelled, spiked dead leaves that littered the ground beneath were a danger to hands and feet when the place was being tidied up.

I felt some affinity with the monkey-puzzle. It, too, was the only specimen in its environment and content just to happily exist, sipping the rain in winter, standing firm against the buffeting March gales, shedding its worn out clothing to be gathered up by others and in

2

summer sending out fresh shoots of a beguiling green. At the base of this largely unadmired tree grew an abundance of lilac, mauve, purple and white making the air heady with scent in late spring days.

The path from the front gate to the steps was under a rickety wooden pergola which in summer held a profusion of pale pink "Dorothy Perkins" roses. This was the choice of my grandmother, although Gramps always groused about them, calling them a "nuisance rose" as they were subject to bud rot, spiders and other ills, and he felt Grannie would be better served with a nice evergreen covering for her walkway.

The front door opened on to a long, narrow hall, floored with green linoleum and sprinkled with slip mats on which the grandchildren used to slide with shrieks of joy, pretending to be on the Cresta Run.

Locomotion for ordinary mortals was fraught with danger as the passage was always highly polished and many an unwary stranger stepping into the hall would find a mat taking off like greased lightening, depositing him or her on their backs, legs in air in a most undignified position.

In vain did the family plead with Grannie and Gramps to have the hall carpeted, fearing that the old people themselves would take a tumble. But they never heeded the advice and the hall retained its treacherous surface for all of their tenure.

The stairs faced the front door and were a focal point for the grandchildren for the walls were hung with large, framed cartoons of the Napoleonic wars, the drawings grotesque with heads and arms and legs and cannon balls flying in all directions. My two boy cousins and myself had hours of entertainment deciphering the captions in their tiny copperplate writing and delighting in the carnage.

The stairs also proved one of the most intriguing part of the house to decorate at Christmas, and grandchildren staying were given free rein to their imagination in this matter. This came to an abrupt end one year when, armed with Grannie's leather gardening gloves, alone and untended, I twined large holly boughs in and out of the banisters, planting a small tree in a pot at the bottom which made both ascent and descent a lethal exercise and I was commanded to remove the offending greenery forthwith.

The banisters ran straight from top to bottom, impossible not to get astride and slide down their polished oaken length, wooshing off at the bottom to land in a heap of giggles on a mat that promptly shot off at a tangent. Both my cousins and myself had been forbidden to slide down the banister rail, and my eldest cousin Tom, nine years my senior, soon got too grand to join in the fun but his brother Paddy, his junior by three years, and myself for some years availed ourselves of this method of rapid and venturesome descent, often getting caught and suffering a tiresome monologue of the immodesty of such behaviour from whichever adult arrived on the scene.

The hall led from the front to the back door and round the corner at the far end to the kitchen. At one time there had been a modest, spring mounted, green baize door cutting off the front from the back of the house. This had been removed after it had slammed shut on an unwary parlour-maid bearing a tureen of soup to the dining room. Result, a scalded maid, a smashed tureen from the best service and no soup for dinner.

In the far left hand corner of the long passage, in front of the second door to the dining room and before you came to the back door or ventured on to the kitchen, stood a dumb waiter and a large copper gong, the latter rung diligently by the parlour-maid to summon the family to meals.

Gramps would be waiting for the "off" each time, his gold hunter held firmly in his hand, watching the hour hand fall into place. It was always a source of interest to visitors as to why the sounding of the gong was necessary when he was so obviously on the starting blocks at the appointed hour. However, should the gong sound even one minute late, my grandfather would snort and exclaim "Dinner's late, what have those girls been up to?"

Inside the front door and on the left hand wall hung an oak framed barometer, which Gramps religiously tapped each morning before going into breakfast, informing all those gathered for the repast what the weather was going to be like for the next twenty four hours.

There was a large, heavy oak hallstand with lots of carving, and a mirror set in the back. This piece of furniture held all the visible signs of those who inhabited the house. On the pegs were Grannie's wide-brimmed straw gardening hat, Gramps's greening bowler worn to church on Sundays, for occasional trips to London or for weddings and funerals, several tweed caps and a scarf or two.

A large Ulster, given to Gramps by his children on his 50th birthday, was black and stiff, weighed a ton and covered him from head to heel as if in a shroud. He used to laugh and say, "it will see me out", and so it proved, giving over 40 years protection from cold and wet. Hanging modestly beside this Leviathan of a garment was Grannie's lightweight mackintosh, used in the garden or for walks, all her coats being kept upstairs.

The stand held a selection of sticks, each with its own story. We were totally barred from handling the sword stick which Gramps had bought in Germany in the 1880s and whose innocent black exterior contained a gleaming stiletto-type knife.

One bamboo stick had a knobbly head, which, when twisted and pulled upwards, revealed a beautifully calibrated brass measuring rod for horses, which could accommodate an equine up to 18 hands. It had been used in the days when my grandfather had his own hunters and carriage horses. We like this stick and used to cajole Gramps into measuring us with it. I preferred being measured in "hands" rather than boring old inches, recorded by Grannie on the edge of the dining room door; she measured all her grandchildren during their growing years.

Another stick came from Switzerland and was painted with little coloured scenes. There was a very elegant stick with a carved ivory handle used by my grandmother on visits to town. Her modest walking stick, in daily use, had a sensible curved handle which proved its worth on annual blackberrying expeditions.

The cream linen sunshade with the green lining, under which my mother and grandmother took turns to sit when taking afternoon tea on the lawn in summer, nestled companionably with Gramps's correctly rolled black umbrella, its silver band inscribed with his initials and the date of his 21st birthday.

A separate hook at the side held three hunting whips with bone handles and long lashes and a dog chain on which the wily Sealyham, Michael, was taken for his daily walks. A leather lead was useless as he would chomp through it with one swipe of his mighty jaws and hi-tail it off after the paper boy's bicycle or the last horseman to pass the house, however long ago that might have been. Michael was the eternal optimist.

The drawer in the hall stand contained his brush and comb but few ever attempted to use these on him, and he lived a blissfully scruffy life with a full complement of fleas and a few patches of eczema in hot weather, until, that is, my mother and I arrived, then he would be caught, muzzled, stripped, bathed and have his nails cut, much to his disgust, and as soon as free would rush outside to roll in the nearest flower bed to get back to normal!

The drawer also contained his worm pills which no-one had ever able to force down his reluctant throat, so they were secreted in his dinner, only to be spat out when his highly developed taste buds told him of alien things in his food.

7

Grannie's leather gardening gloves also lived in the drawer, together with her secateurs, sundry pieces of lampwick, little coils of string, a pair of old scissors, a discarded corkscrew, a variety of keys, a few corks and some drawing pins.

The polished top of the drawer held a small silver salver for the morning post and for the visiting cards of the many people who came to call.

# CHAPTER
## TWO

# They Came to Call

Calling was still very much in vogue in country districts in the 1920s and '30s, and a great many characters trooped through the hall to the drawing room.

Due to the enthusiasm for highly polished linoleum and slip mats, not all had an easy passage. One visit was from the vicar, a portly man whose feet went from under him and he ended up in the arms of the parlour-maid who had opened the door, to the great embarrassment of both parties.

Then there was the lady in high heels who missed one of the three steps down into the drawing room and fell in the tea trolley. However, most made the transition from front door to drawing room without mishap.

One of the delightful characters who came to call was Mrs Sugden who still wore Edwardian dresses and large hats, and arrived in a landau pulled by a very old mare and driven by an even older coachman in a cocked hat, while under the carriage a vintage Dalmatian trotted sedately.

Mrs Sugden lived in a large, wisteria covered, grey stone house at the end of the village. She was a close friend of my grandmother, and often sent the carriage to collect her for afternoon tea. I loved being included in these trips, even if it did mean wearing the hated hat and gloves, because not only was the landau such a lovely mode of travel, but because Mrs Sugden had such an interesting house.

She and her husband had lived in many strange countries and the house was full of the extraordinary things brought back from their travels.

Apart from that Mrs Sugden owned three parrots, who were to be found in cages in the grand conservatory. They had been given to her by a sailor nephew and could not be left in the house when visitors were expected owing to their colourful language. I was always allowed to run out to see them but never succeeded in getting them to say anything except "Hello Polly" and "She's an old trout." To whom the parrot was referring I have no idea.

I also visited the stables with the clock tower, where white fan-tailed pigeons strutted on the tiled roof, to give the ancient mare slices of carrot and pat the old dog who dozed in the sunshine.

Mrs Sugden died when I was about eleven and in her Will left me a book on garden flowers.

Mr and Mrs Thursby were also frequent visitors and came in a highly polished Daimler. They lived in a long, low house in a large park outside the village, and Grannie often took me on the return call which was made in the village taxi.

I loved this house because it was set in green lawns with old spreading cedar trees, and there were peacocks who cried mournfully all during tea and would come to the French windows to take biscuits from my fingers. Sadly all these lovely birds were one by one killed by the foxes who proliferated in the area.

Two spinster sisters lived at the end of our road and frequently walked down to take tea. There were a number of middle-aged unmarried ladies living in the district, most of them had lost fiancés in the Great War and remained single and true to their first loves.

The Misses Carter were two such. The story I was told when I was older was that they had become engaged to two brothers who had perished on the Somme. They were well upholstered jolly ladies, and I often went to see them and the younger Miss Carter and I went for long walks on the commons and in the woods.

Miss Ludlam lived opposite Foxhill in another imposing house in several acres of garden surrounded by an eight foot high wooden wall. She was a great gardener and had everything from rose to primula gardens, a sunken area with a stream and waterfalls, a shrubbery and a bamboo plantation.

Although she had a full time gardener with a boy to help him, Miss Ludlam spent most of her life on her knees in the flower beds. She owned a small black Schipperke called Pip, who spent all day racing up and down the wall yapping furiously in case anyone happened to be passing. He and Michael loathed each other and the noise when we passed on our afternoon walk was deafening. I dread to think what would have happened if the two dogs had ever met.

Miss Ludlam, whose Christian name Grannie told us was Lila (no-one was called by their Christian name at that time until both parties had known each other for several years), was tall and slender with bobbed hair and she wore no make up; her elegant country clothes were plain but of impeccable cloth and cut. She was a daily visitor and the family used to laughingly call her Gramps's "lady friend", as he lent her his copy of the *Financial Times* and they exchanged racing tips.

One of Miss Ludlam's brothers was stationed in India and sent his only daughter back home to boarding school. Before term started Paula came to stay for a week with her aunt and I was invited over to play.

Paula, a stocky ten year old with tanned face and limbs and short bobbed black hair, was a monster, spoiled by her Ayah to whom she constantly referred. She was as wild as a monkey and behaved like one, swarming up trees and dropping on me unexpectedly, or hanging off a branch to grab my long hair with which she endeavoured to lift me off the ground. I was no weakling and we had some good scraps. I went home after the first visit with two quite severe bruises on my arm caused by her biting me. When questioned as to how I came by these marks I told the truth, as I had been taught; strangely no-one would believe me as Paula showed such a demure face in front of the adults. So each day I had to go over and play with Paula and I was most thankful when the week came to an end. I often wondered how they coped with her at school.

The two Miss Griffiths were leftovers from an even earlier age than Mrs Sugden, looking as if they had never left the Victorian era with their trailing skirts and flower trimmed bonnets. They arrived and left in the village taxi, and everyone groaned when it was known they had arrived for tea, as they were prissy in the extreme and had little conversation apart from the arrangement of flowers in the little Mission church, the difficulty of keeping a maid and how cheeky the local children were getting.

The Major and his sister lived on the opposite side of the lane to the Misses Carter, in a house on the corner, one side shielded from the main road and the Rising Sun Inn by a wooden wall and a plantation of trees. They were wizened, parchment coloured people, as if they had quite dried out in the heat of the plains of India, where the Major served for many years, and where his sister had lived and cared for him.

Their house too was full of interesting things, a tiger skin rug filled the small hall and nearly everyone, at some time, tripped over its mounted head. The Major had rowed for Cambridge in his college days, and his oar was displayed on the wall at the head of the stairs and bore the signatures of the triumphant crew; it was flanked by his cap and other mementoes of his youth.

These two elderly people walked down the lane to Foxhill and rustled in at the front door and into the drawing room with a sound like dried grass in a breeze. The Major's voice, which no doubt once resounded round the parade ground, was reduced to a breathy rasp, as he ground on with stories of the regiment, punctuating his memories with words like "jemidar" and "havildar" which intrigued me as I had no idea to whom or what he referred, while his sister put in little asides in a soft whisper.

The Greenstreets lived next to the Major and were regular callers in the 1920s. Mr Greenstreet was full of knowledge about the countryside, and I spent some interesting times in their house which had an extensive library, looking at books on this subject in which I was keenly interested, and being fed lemonade and cake by Mrs Greenstreet. They were both quite elderly and Mr Greenstreet suffered a stroke from which he did not recover and he too left me a book in his Will. It was called *"The Outdoor World"* and became my bible for all the years I collected bugs and beetles, moths and birds' eggs, mosses and wild flowers and pails of newts and tadpoles from the dewponds on the common.

Mrs Greenstreet moved away and Grannie only called once on the new occupants of their house who happened to be out at the time, so she left her cards, but no return call was ever paid.

The new occupants were a bright, brassy young woman with a shifty eyed husband and several children. It was whispered in the village that "er was very modern and one of them there vegetarians", and that they sunbathed in very little if anything on in the way of clothes. Who started the whispers was unclear.

Certainly Mr King, whose house lay between their house and our meadow, would not have said anything, indeed if he had seen anything of the sort he would have been far too embarrassed to mention it. Mr King called mainly to see Gramps and to discuss gardening matters, as he was a great rose grower. A shy bachelor of advancing years, he could only occasionally be persuaded to come into the drawing room for tea.

Another caller was Mrs Kirkwood, a lady in her early forties, very smart and stylish, with black shingled hair and a great deal of lipstick. Grannie was not fond of her and Gramps vanished as soon as her car drove up to the gate and he saw the liveried chauffeur handing her out. She had two sons at Wellington and used to come and collect Grannie and anyone else she could decoy into her car each spring when the boys were on manoeuvres on the common, as both were officer cadets.

It was a most boring outing as we sat waiting for something to happen, which it never did, but the whole afternoon seemed to give Mrs Kirkwood incredible satisfaction and she never ceased to be bubbling over with praise for "her boys" who were, in her eyes, so wonderful. Sometimes they were brought to tea with her during the holidays and I thought them dreadfully dreary, for one wore wire rimmed spectacles, both were thin and anaemic looking and they had no conversation.

Miss Miles was another of Gramps's "lady friends". She lived near Mrs Sugden in a pretty white, rose-covered house set up a side lane, and she bred and exhibited White Beveran rabbits with great success. She and Gramps (who bred Blue Beverans) always had much to talk about and were great rivals in the showing world. One year Miss Miles annoyed Gramps, who had always supplied me with pet rabbits, by giving me a white doe of very uncertain temperament who would come for you with claws and teeth when the hutch door was opened. This earned for her the sobriquet "Mrs Maggie Bun Snorter". In spite of her unpleasant habits, I was devoted to this handsome rodent and had her for some years. She got quite used to our changes of location, and even accompanied us to Foxhill much to the disgust of my grandfather!

The church was situated in the village proper at the bottom of a long hill, and the Common was served by a Mission Church and a sad curate. The vicar, who lived in some style near his church, only paid occasional visits to his flock who lived on the Common, and the village grapevine usually managed to alert those who dwelt there of his impending visit.

He was a portly man, red faced who drank his tea with a slurping noise. Gramps used to ask him awkward Biblical questions, to some of which he had no answer, so his teatime visits were mercifully short. There was a twinkle in Gramps's eye as the vicar departed, usually somewhat hurriedly.

Near neighbours who never called, nor did Grannie call on them, lived up a long drive about a quarter of a mile past Foxhill. On one afternoon walk when we were accompanied by Gramps, I asked him who lived up the long drive. He snorted and said "That grocer fella!" I learned later their name was Sainsbury!

Most welcome visitors were relations who came in a steady stream through the year, some for lunch or tea, some to stay.

Although mother's brother, Uncle G, was a much loved visitor, it was their younger sister, Aunt Lovey, who brought fun and laughter into the house.

There were relations from overseas, from Wales and the Home Counties, cousins and second cousins and some, Grannie told me, were "once or twice removed". I studied these latter quite carefully but they looked quite normal to me!

# CHAPTER
# THREE

# Treasures in the Study

The focal point of Gramps's study was the big, oak roll-top desk, always piled with letters, Suttons seed catalogues, rabbit and poultry show schedules, appeals from charities, order forms for spring bulbs, livestock labels, balls of gardening twine, interesting newspaper cuttings, live cartridges, spent cartridges, the odd mousetrap and so on.

The top of the desk boasted a spill holder which I had made for him one Christmas from a cocoa tin, some scraps of wallpaper and some gimp; if I had given him the Koh-i-Noor he could not have been more pleased. This monument to my lack of artistic talent was filled with spills which I had been taught to fold from discarded newspapers and were used by Gramps to light his pipe from any handy flame and thus save matches. The holder also contained the chicken wing feathers which were snipped straight at the top and so made ready to ream out his pipes.

The rack of favourite pipes in various stages of use hung above the desk together with a five year calendar still displaying January 1st of the year my cousins gave it to him, and a letter rack, which Gramps had fashioned from strips of wood. The letters contained in this were covered in dust and yellow with age and to my knowledge had never been referred to since they were first opened.

Gramps was not a great letter writer but when he did reply to a missive he believed in not wasting paper, folding the letter carefully at the bottom of the writer's signature and then neatly slicing off the unused piece of the sheet and penning his reply on this morsel in his cramped hand.

My grandfather had enjoyed a very full life. Like all Victorian gentleman of means he had travelled a good deal in his younger days, was of an enquiring turn of mind and had dabbled in collecting many things: coins, stamps, birds' eggs, moths and butterflies, to name but a few.

He had been a keen amateur geologist and a multitude of various coloured rocks and stones of strange shapes and sizes were strewn about the study, used as paperweights, bookends and door stop. Surplus stones crowded the mantelpiece, spilled off shelves filling every nook or cranny available. There was also a glass display case in which some of the best and, presumably, valuable were set out, carefully labelled with date and place of discovery.

A velvet lined case displayed rare old coins, a cabinet housed the birds' eggs, while the moths and butterflies, once captured in the large net standing behind the door in company with an alpenstock, a keep net and rods in cotton sleeves, were fixed in frames and hanging on the walls.

Over the mantelpiece in a glass case was the salmon he caught in Scotland at his first attempt. Behind the door was suspended his fishing creel, two canvas game bags, a bandolier to hold cartridges and the large brimmed hat with a veil left over from the days when he kept a thriving apiary.

Two mounted fox masks snarled menacingly from either side of the marble mantelpiece above a grate in which a fire was never lit, not even in the coldest weather. The antlers of a stag bagged on another Scottish expedition were impaled above the desk.

My grandfather had always been a great owner of animals and at Foxhill. He not only kept his stud of rabbits but several pens of pedigree poultry who had also won many awards. Specimens of both were put into travelling boxes each weekend and dispatched by rail to shows the length and breadth of the land.

Prize cards of every denomination were everywhere in the study, pushed in picture frames, crammed into pigeon holes in the desk, on the mantelpiece stuck in bunches behind various lumps of stone, vying with the discarded letters behind the blue-veined marble clock whose sonorous voice told out the hours and competed for accuracy with the grandfather clock in the dining room.

Much of Gramps's time was taken up with gardening at which he was expert and what with that, his poultry and rabbits and his ceaseless war against the predators, foxes, stoats, weasels, birds, mice and rats that threatened his livestock, their feedstuffs or his garden produce, he led a very full life and the study was its reflection.

On wet days I used to wheedle Gramps into turning out one or two of the pigeon holes in the desk or one of the drawers in the pedestals supporting its frame. Letters from long dead cousins, old silk greetings cards, out of date game licences, invitations never accepted, all in a delightful jumble.

Best of all were the faded Victorian photographs depicting Gramps on Mont Blanc with tweed hat, knickerbockers and alpenstock, Gramps on the family yacht clad in yachting cap at a jaunty angle, white ducks and dark blazer, Gramps in a group at a shooting party, the bag of birds spread out in neat lines, Gramps landing a fish and one of him up a tree taking a swarm of bees. Many pictures of the family picnicking, the men in high stiff collars and boaters, striped blazers and white trousers, the ladies in long, muslin, full-skirted dresses and huge straw hats laden with flowers.

One drawer contained several intricately carved Meerschaum pipes brought back from a German holiday and carefully preserved in tissue paper. The desk was a never ending source of delight.

My favourite perch in the study was the window seat from which, with Michael beside me, we could observe anyone coming to, or going past the house, always an excitement as I wondered whose was the strange car (few passed at the time), where the coal cart was going and when the pony and trap driven by the old lady who sold delicious, rich, creamy-yellow home made ice cream, would arrive.

When the clanging of her brass bell echoed down the lane, Cook would appear with a large earthenware bowl and, for the princely sum of two shillings, Gramps would have it filled to the brim from the tub wrapped in sacking that was securely wedged in the little cart. The ice cream, divided equally among family and staff, was Gramps's treat to us every week in summer.

A large polished pine chest stood in front of the window seat; when opened it displayed a wonderful collection of carpenter's tools, all in beautiful condition. This was not because they saw little use, on the contrary, they were always being called to duty, but because Gramps was meticulous in cleaning and polishing any tool used. This applied equally to the garden tools as well as those in the box, from a garden fork to a screwdriver, keeping them clean and well oiled and always returned to their own niche in box or shed when their work was completed.

We all loved this box of treasures, but because some were sharp we were not allowed to take them out unless Gramps was supervising. He taught us the names of all the tools and their uses, and as they were continually in use we were able to observe their work for ourselves.

On a small, square table to the right of the window stood one of Gramps's most prized possessions, the barograph or aneroid barometer which had belonged to his father. This contraption, housed under a glass cover, consisted of two copper drums and slender brass arms with points through which ink flowed. It recorded the barometric pressure on a piece of paper secured round the drums which revolved slowly leaving the delicate ink-tipped arms to make uncertain, wavering lines for interpretation by the owner. It was a great day when the paper ran out and had to be replaced by a fresh roll and the glass case was removed for this interesting operation.

On another table stood a small spirit stove, a kettle and a much scorched cloth pot holder embroidered with lurid roses in cross stitch by my step-sister when she was a child and given to Gramps one birthday. It had stood the test of time and several fires and explosions as well.

Gramps was always boiling up something noxious on this stove using an old chipped, enamel saucepan rescued from the kitchen where its three pot menders in the bottom had eventually deemed it unfit for use. The fact that the stove frequently caught fire, the saucepan boiled over or the whole thing just blew up, only heightened the excitement of the adventures we had, and all Gramps's grandchildren would egg him on to try some experiment in the hope that some sudden and unexpected but longed for drama would take place.

Once he tried making fireworks and set the drab, green curtains alight, extinguishing the flames with the contents of the saucepan. These drapes were never replaced as my grandmother remarked severely that if he would indulge in such childish pranks he did not deserve new curtains. For all the rest of my childhood the green, scorched hangings remained unrepentant. To me they were a monument to the fun we had when

Gramps was willing to be urged to try another experiment. When things went wrong he would roar with laughter and shout "Worse things happen at sea!" and I believe it is him I have to thank for my philosophical attitude when life gets difficult.

A side table held a collection of bottles and jugs for Gramps distilled all manner of herbs, drinking the liquid prepared with evident relish and satisfactory remarks such as "That's the stuff to give the troops!" No-one else in the family would touch these concoctions and my mother was convinced that one day he would poison himself, but he lived for 93 happy, healthy years, visiting neither dentist, oculist or doctor, only being attended by the "quack", as he called the latter, when on occasions my grandmother deemed it essential, such as when he fell out of an apple tree at the age of 86 and knocked himself out and so had no say in the matter!

His favourite potion was made from the flowers of the Common Centaury, one of dozens of lovely herbs that grew in meadows before the permanent pastures were all ploughed up and chemicals used on the land. The Centaury grew to a height of about twelve inches and had bright pink blossoms. I used to be dispatched over to the Stile Field to gather bunches of this plant. This narrow strip of meadowland was bisected by a footpath that led from our lane to the back of the village and had a stile each end, hence the name.

When I returned with a good bunch of Centaury it would be thrust head down into a large rose-decorated jug with a fluted lip, and when the kettle boiled the

24

water was poured on to the flower heads filling the jug to the brim.

There it stayed for days and days, the liquid getting darker and smelling more brackish, until Gramps threw away the withered flowers, strained the liquid and then bottled it. A number of these infusions were made during the months when the herb flowered and these kept him going all the year until the plant blossomed the next summer. I once allowed him to give me a taste; it was awful, so bitter. He rocked with laughter at my disgusted expression and the fact that I spat the offending mouthful into my handkerchief and he told me I would never grow up to have his stamina!

Bookcases occupied the corner positions on the right beyond the window. They contained, apart from a Bradshaw and the slender telephone directory, old dusty tomes on coal mining and iron foundries in Wales all of which had connections with the family wealth in past generations, wealth that had been dissipated in later years.

There was a book entitled "*Games for Boys*" printed around 1840, a number of books on the countryside, plants, birds and insects as well as all manner of country sports and pursuits, many manuals on poultry and rabbit keeping and one on taxidermy, which Gramps had once taken up with great enthusiasm, so I was told, as it was before my days. Grannie put a stop to this when rather smelly carcasses appeared indoors!

I rather liked the large illustrated volumes recounting the details of important gentlemen in Glamorganshire in the second half of the 19th century. They were pictured side-whiskered or bearded and very earnest, their eyes bulging with the height and stiffness of their collars and the tightness of their ties.

There were two or three Holy Bibles and a beautiful set of Shakespeare's plays in three gold-leaved volumes, bound in Moroccan leather, which Gramps gave me in my early teens when he found I had a passion for the Bard. There were no novels or reading books as such, as Gramps relied on Boots Lending Library for the latest detective fiction which he devoured avidly each evening.

The faded Turkish carpet was seldom brushed, Gramps did not like the maids in his study, he said they disturbed his papers and he could not find anything after they had cleaned up, so the dust settled happily on everything, and when he wanted a book or paper he would give a great puff and blow the dust off, laughing as Michael and I sneezed at the resulting cloud.

The big, sash window like all those downstairs in the old part of the house had heavy wooden shutters which each night were religiously closed and fastened by a large steel bar. The fact that in the newer portion of the house the more modern windows of similar style had no such protection did not deter Gramps from taking precautions against intruders as he thought fit.

One other item in the study was unique, the telephone. My grandparents fought a rearguard action against their children who pressed them continually to avail themselves of the latest modern marvel, but for many years they remained adamant. One year my grandmother was taken ill with a gall bladder infection and it was necessary to reach the family quickly and Miss Ludlam's telephone was used. After this they relented and a prim, polished board was screwed to the wall between the bookcase and the window, and on this was mounted an arm with spring holder that held the telephone, black and menacing, and only to be used in times of dire adversity.

That their children rang with messages of goodwill at Christmas and birthdays was considered an arrant waste of money. I learned many years later, through my cousin Paddy who had a keen nose for ferreting out family secrets, that Gramps used to wait until Grannie went into the garden to cut flowers and would then stealthily shut the door to the study and communicate in hushed tones with his bookmaker!

No-one in the village, which was large as villages go but very spread out, could, up to then, have taken to the telephone in a big way as Gramps's number was a modest "45".

I was terrified of this monster out of whose black depth strange metallic voices came from who-knows-where, and I could never be induced to speak into it, and if made to listen to a message from some relative, stood as far away as possible.

None of the maids would answer its urgent bell; in fact, when they were without visitors, my grandfather was the only person who touched it.

# CHAPTER
# FOUR

# Two Logs and the Salmon Cutlet

The long dining room with windows either end, facing north and south, was a room of many parts as all manner of interesting things took place there. My mother hated the dining room as it was always so cold, even in summer, no doubt in some measure because it was situated over the cellars.

When my grandparents bought Foxhill this room had been two, one the dining room and the other the sitting room. My grandparents had the dividing wall knocked down making one large room, and built on a new drawing room.

When alterations were carried out, the fireplace in the original dining room was removed, leaving the one from the old sitting room to service a much bigger area. This grate was not only very small but most inconveniently sited being right opposite the door into the hall and beside the archway leading to the three steps down into the new drawing room.

In the cast-iron basket that sat demurely in the tiled grate it was not permitted to burn coal; that would have been considered a great waste by my grandfather who instead provided logs cut from fallen trees, the long two-handled saw necessary to produce such fuel being wielded by Gramps and John, the garden boy.

Only two logs appeared to be smouldering at any one time, and my Aunt Lovey, mother's younger sister, who never minded what she said to the father who adored her, would remark that she was sure they were the same two logs that had been there the last time she stayed.

Most of these logs were of pine, there being heather-clad commons nearby on which this species proliferated and in the winter gales many were blown down, bringing others of their ilk down with them. Pine logs, even with little or no encouragement to burn brightly, do tend to ignite fairly easily, and once they have done so send out showers of pretty sparks, which no doubt accounted for the many scorch marks on the hearth rug.

Michael liked to sit on this rug and receive whatever warmth there might be, and in winter his thick white coat was marked in places with yellow where sparks had jumped out and singed him, although it never appeared to worry him in the slightest.

At each end of the mantelpiece stood a solid brass figure of a scantily clad gentleman struggling with a rearing stallion, and in the middle a beautiful French clock under a glass dome, its movement being a graduated brass spindle affair jutting from back to front from which a waxed string unwound itself over eight days. Every Sunday the glass cover on the French clock was removed and carefully cleaned by Gramps and the clock rewound with a delicate brass key. No-one else ever touched this treasure.

On the recessed wall to the right of the fireplace hung a huge picture, the Westall, so called after the artist who painted it. It was an enormous gold framed panorama of a galleon in full sail on stormy, white capped seas and was Gramps's pride and joy as he loved the sea and ships. This view was not shared by my grandmother who had spent the first few months of her married life strapped in her bunk in the family yacht while it ploughed through Westall-like waves to sundry foreign parts.

My mother, who was terribly bad sailor, refused to look at the picture as she said it made her feel sea-sick. My boy cousins thought it splendid, the younger because it suggested adventure and excitement and the elder because it was valuable and represented cash in hand!

The painting on the wall by the window was my favourite, a beautiful copy of "*The Horse Fair*" by Rosa Bonheur. Many artists copied this towering picture of horseflesh, and this was a particularly good copy. It had been given to my great-grandfather in the 19th century, and I always hoped that one day it would come down to me, although I would scarcely ever have had a wall big enough to accommodate it. Sadly, many years later it passed out of the main branch of the family into the hands of a distant cousin.

The picture that was the joy and delight of the younger members of the family and Auntie Lovey, but the abomination of my mother, hung on a section of wall which jutted out where the two rooms had been divided, a shrewd placing as it fortunately could not be seen by the diners. It was known to the family as "*The Salmon Cutlet*", and depicted the decapitated body of John the Baptist, severed neck to the forefront (hence our title for this masterpiece) with Salome holding up the head by its hair while it dripped blood into a salver held by a serving man. A number of family jokes surrounded this picture, and the younger members watched with glee the faces of visitors after they had given them a viewing.

The fourth large picture in the room was another good copy, that of a Stubbs, just one thoroughbred racehorse in a stable, which hung over the mantelpiece. Of course there were a number of smaller pictures, one frame held four signed miniatures by Baxter which today hangs in my sitting room.

The furniture was immense. The mahogany dining table filling the centre of the room with six leather-buttoned chairs on either side. On hot summer days small girls' thighs stuck agonisingly to the leather and had to be carefully prized loose at the end of the meal.

At one end was a gentleman's "Carver" with large curly ended arms, and at the other a similar chair of rather more graceful proportions for the lady of the house.

The highly polished surface of the table was always protected by a dull crimson cloth in some heavy material, fringed with bobbles. Set centre, a bowl of flowers in spring and summer and in autumn and winter an Aladdin lamp, a large, oil burning illuminator covered by a mushroom-shaped pearly glass shade.

For meals the whole table was covered by a pristine white linen tablecloth with similar napkins, which, when clean, were made into the shape of ships in full sail but once used, consigned to the napkin holder of each family member. A silver ring deftly chased with swallows and roses and engraved with her initials for Grannie, an ivory ring set with his initials for Gramps, a plain silver ring for my mother and a heavy wooden six sided one for me.

The silver was old and heavy and the forks lethal, many a visitor inadvertently stabbing mouth or gum with their sharp prongs. The knives were steel, worn of blade and shining from the daily burnishing given them by John. No stainless steel was ever allowed in the house.

An immense oak sideboard was set against the wall opposite the fire. It had a high carved back in which was framed an oval mirror, and a top supported by the figures of two knights in full armour, leaning on swords embedded in the ground, and with downcast heads and closed eyes. My aunt used to say that they had probably consumed the stewed rhubarb that appeared daily on the table all through the year!

A large walnut Tantalus embossed in silver held three cut glass decanters, various labelled "Brandy", "Whisky" and "Rum" on little silver shields hanging on chains round their necks; there was never more than an inch of liquid in any of the bottles. My grandparents were very abstemious, spirits were there only in a purely medicinal capacity.

Some interesting pieces of silver were displayed on the sideboard, a twin sugar holder won by my grandparents for archery, and a set of salt cellars four inches across, encrusted with acanthus leaves and lions' heads and feet.

I have sat enthralled at lunch watching unsuspecting visitors ladling salt over their stewed rhubarb from these cellars, mistakenly thinking they contained sugar! It says much for the manners of the day that these hapless wretches somehow managed to down much of this unpalatable dish without a murmur.

Gramps would sometimes notice what was going on and say nothing, simply grinning under his moustache and giving me a huge wink. However, if Grannie noticed she quietly called for another fruit bowl from the hovering maid. Visitors might avoid the salt but there was no excuse for not eating the rhubarb!

The cutlery was kept in a large oak canteen beside the far door into the hall which was blocked by a large piece of shelved furniture with ornate legs and curly feet. On its shelves stood the silver entree dishes used for holding the vegetables, and either so scalding hot that you burned your fingers, or so cold the vegetables within had become a flaccid, tepid mass. The behaviour of these dishes depended totally on the temper of the cook at that particular repast.

My mother once suggested that this piece of furniture should be moved and the door made practical, it would be a shorter distance for the maid to carry the dishes, as it was she had to come up the hall and in at the top door. The suggestion was reluctantly agreed to and implemented, the dish holder going to stand under the Westall. However, for some reason the grandparents decided the top door suited them better and things rapidly returned to normal.

Under the south window another sizeable table was covered by a crimson cloth. In winter this housed Gramps's geraniums in enormous pots. They were really giant plants standing almost three feet high having resisted all attempts to prune them to a reasonable size, and they completely blocked out any shafts of the pale wintry sun.

Grannie was not a lover of geraniums as she did not care for their smell, but Gramps was totally addicted, and every autumn, before the frosts came, the plants were once more dug up, returned to their pots and carefully carried back into the dining room. In the corner made by the jutting piece of the original wall, and set sideways to the Salmon Cutlet, was the Grandfather Clock which like the mantel clock was conscientiously wound up each Sunday morning. It worked by a system of pulleys and weights, had been in the family for years and its imperious voice told the hours and the quarters all through my childhood. Strangely, as the old song goes, it really did stop "when the old man died", and no-one was able to get it to go again.

On the south wall there was a built-in corner cupboard from floor to ceiling. No doubt due to the warmth generated by the sun on the wall and no thanks to any indoor heating, it was a Mecca for those little beetles called "silver fish" that live and thrive in warm dark places. The china lived with the silver fish and to be asked to fetch extra plates and cups when unexpected callers arrived at tea time meant a quick swipe at the beetles before those for whom the china was destined noticed the unwelcome inhabitants!

The dining room's day began early in the morning when the maids came down and the house parlour-maid cleaned the grate and in winter started the two logs on their way. She then set about the carpet with the Bissell broom, flicked a quick duster over the furniture and laid the breakfast table, before taking up early tea trays to the bedrooms.

Breakfast was a slightly protracted meal and rather more of a ritual then the others. For instance my grandmother took the head of the table, a place occupied by Gramps for lunch and dinner, so that she had room to preside over the making of the coffee. The percolator consisted of two pieces of glassware fitted one inside the other, water in the bottom container warmed by the flame of a little glass holder containing methylated spirit, the coffee was in the vase shaped top. After a while the water boiled and burst upwards with delighted chuckles engulfing the waiting grounds that had been ladled in from a tin of "Red, White and Blue", then one of the popular brands.

Grannie arrived in the dining room at precisely ten minutes to nine. The morning papers and the post would be neatly laid beside her plate. This early arrival gave her time to get the coffee process started, to sort out the letters for the various addressees and to scan the headlines of the *Daily Express*, before the arrival of the rest of the family who would have been summoned by the urgent voice of the gong.

Gramps had already been out early to see to the traps set for the mice and rats, and to check on the garden and the weather as well as set John his tasks for early morning.

As soon as everyone was present my grandfather pronounced the Grace that preceded all meals, "For what we are about to receive may the Lord make us truly thankful", and we all sat down. Grannie handed out the post and everyone opened their letters and, if interesting or from a family member, read pieces to everyone whether they wanted to hear them or not.

Should there be any parcels all were opened under Gramps's watchful eye. He hated waste of any sort, and insisted that adults as well as children open parcels in the correct manner so as not to waste string or paper, and everyone obeyed; it was easier than trying to circumvent him.

The person to whom the parcel was addressed was instructed how to unpick the knots in the string which bound the whole together, bearing in mind that there was no such thing as Sellotape in those days. Most of the knots had been very tightly tied and were sometimes covered in red sealing wax which first had to be scraped off. Gramps would help with the knots, easing them apart with the point of his giant pocket knife. Once the string was removed and straightened out, it had to be wound round the hand in a skein, then twisted and fastened with the free end. It was then time to take off the brown paper which had to be smoothed and folded tidily before the next stage.

As people at that time packed their parcels carefully there were often several layers of various types of paper each secured with fine string or coloured tape or ribbon, before one actually got to the contents. Oh! the agony of trying to get the knots undone, the wait while the packaging was dealt with when one was just longing to find out just what the parcel contained.

The adults suffered in the same way. Perhaps we appreciated the contents more after all this travail and I must say when anyone in the house wanted to pack a parcel there was always a quantity of smooth brown paper and knot-free string from which to choose!

Fragrant coffee was dispensed in the large willow pattered breakfast cups, and an extra large cup for Gramps who relished this drink with much lip smacking and whisker sucking; this ritual succeeded the consumption of any favoured beverage, a performance that irritated Grannie greatly although she never mentioned it, her expression said it all.

Grannie had porridge for breakfast all year round and into it she put a variety of things, Bemax, of which Gramps was most scornful, "What do you want to eat that rubbish for, Ivy?" he would say knowing how she disliked this abbreviation of her real name, Isabel, guessing he could not get a rise out of his determined wife but always willing to try. On top of the Bemax went the sliced banana or apples, orange, sometimes grapes, soft fruit when in season and even some of the ever present stewed rhubarb, all liberally sprinkled with salt and mixed with hot milk. Those staying for the first time watched with something akin to horror as my grandmother consumed this plateful with evident relish.

For the rest of us it was bacon and eggs, poached or scrambled eggs, or kippers that had arrived by post in a fish frail from the Isle of Man, sometimes smoked haddock poached in milk or kedgeree, which Gramps refused to eat saying it was a "nasty messed up dish". Strange, as his favourite breakfast was Lava bread, a dark, congealed mass made from seaweed that was posted up from Wales. Cut in pieces and rolled in oatmeal it was fried to a golden brown. I loved it, and Gramps and I happily consumed a dishful under the disbelieving eyes of those gathered at the table.

On Sundays it was always boiled eggs. When I had scraped out the last delicious flake of white, I smashed a hole in the shell so that "the witches could not go to sea", as told by Gramps, for, if you neglected to do this, the witches could sail away in your shell and sink the ships.

The golden toast was held in place by silver toast racks and awaited a variety of home made preserves, marmalade made from the best Seville oranges, and local honey. Gramps, to be different or perhaps just difficult, insisted on a plentiful supply of Green Tomato jam, which he heaped on his toast, telling us every morning that we did not know what we were missing.

Rule for grandchildren was that if we had butter on your toast we could not have marmalade, jam or honey, but if we preferred we could have any of these delights with no butter. Gramps tried to bully the adults into this behaviour, one which he followed most strictly, but mother at least stood firm and had both butter and marmalade. In many ways she was remarkably like him and there was often a clash of their two strong wills.

We sat rather a long time at breakfast for one simple reason: Gramps's teeth, or rather, lack of. By the time he reached his seventies he had lost a great many teeth and they became even fewer as the years rolled on. He resolutely refused to go to a dentist as he would have no truck with dentures. He declared that all people should chew each mouthful of food sixty-five times, and he practised what he preached using his gums, so he took a very long time to consume the two pieces of toast and green tomato jam that rounded off his daily breakfast. He gleefully kept the whole assembly fidgeting until he had concluded his meal and drained his cup with the usual slapping of lips and wiping of the moustaches with his napkin. No-one would have dared leave until the final Grace was said.

Once released the family dispersed like a flock of pigeons. Grannie always had a pressing appointment at ten minutes to ten each day upstairs in the "throne room" as the lavatory was termed, and she departed forthwith, not to be seen again until ten o'clock precisely. By then the maids had cleared the table and the dining room was ready for the next part of the day.

# CHAPTER
# FIVE

# A Room for
# All Seasons

Most dining rooms are pretty sterile, being used
fleetingly for meals and on occasions to entertain
visitors, otherwise being dull and silent places.

The dining room at Foxhill was not like this for it
doubled as a utility room, there being no flower room
on the premises in which various things to do with the
running of the house could be accomplished, so the
dining room was used for all manner of purposes.

Mondays, Wednesdays and Fridays were lamp days.
Tuesday, Thursday and Saturday flower days, and then
there were silver days and china days to be interspersed
in this calendar.

The house had no electricity and was lighted by oil
lamps. On the appointed mornings Grannie would
return to the dining room where she spread newspapers
on the table and the parlour-maid, assisted by myself,
mother and the odd visitor, carried in the lamps from
all over the house and placed them in rows for her
ministrations.

There were two Aladdin lamps whose mantles were so fragile that the wretched things were always breaking and having to be renewed, a very delicate job, and a number of large and small brass lamps with ordinary wicks. All were fitted with glass chimneys and ran on paraffin. Paraffin was contained in a small round can with a very narrow spout. As assistant it was my job to polish the chimneys with a clean, dry washing up mop, getting rid of any smoke stains and finishing with a soft cloth.

Grannie, who had drawn her "lamp gloves" over her slim, long-fingered hands, carefully re-filled all the lamps, from the tiny ones with the white globes that sat in nooks and crannies round the house, hopefully to stop people missing steps and stairs and so falling down and maiming themselves, to the big Aladdins which, if not lighted properly and given time to warm up, flared horribly and filled whichever room they were in with smoke and smuts.

Then Grannie would trim the wicks, cleaning off the soot with a cloth and snipping off loose ends that might cause them to flare. Sometimes one of the maids turned up a lamp too high and it flared and the glass chimney over-heated and went off with a loud pop, usually blowing a hole in the glass, seldom shattering the whole thing. This meant a replacement chimney. The new chimneys were kept out in Gramps's shed, so he had to know about any breakages and made a great fuss about the waste of money incurred!

Once every month all the brass lamps had their chimneys removed early in the morning and were taken into the cellar where John burnished them to a shining brightness.

Once the lamps had all been attended to, I was allowed to help carry them to their respective places. In summer, when lamps were hardly needed, this ritual was only conducted twice a week.

Flower days followed the same pattern, another roll of newspaper covered the table and Grannie donned her gardening gloves. All the vases and bowls were brought from round the house to the dining room. The blooms were lifted from their various containers, sorted over and the dead and dying put in a basket to be taken out and tipped in the compost pit in the vegetable garden. The water was emptied into a tin bucket and the vases refilled from a small galvanised water can.

Now was the time for Grannie to put on her straw hat, adjusting it in the hall-stand mirror and securing it firmly to her head by a long, amber-tipped hat pin. If at all chilly she robed herself in her mackintosh, and should the ground be damp, put on her galoshes.

It was my job to carry the basket and brass handled scissors, one of a set of three, another of my grandparents' prizes won at archery. We surveyed the vast array of flowers in the burgeoning beds and conversed earnestly on what would look best and in which vase.

The spring flowering bulbs, daffodil, narcissus, tulips and snowdrops filled the house from February to April, followed by primroses, wallflowers, Sweet William, forget-me-not, pansies and often bluebells gathered in nearby woods. Honeysuckle took over from branches of yellow catkins and the snowy buds of palm.

By nine years of age I was allowed into the herbaceous border to cut to order the big spikes of blue delphiniums or the many coloured lupins, although I thought this flower a waste of time indoors as it soon drooped, and when revived assumed rather ugly, twisted shapes, and then shed dozens of its hood shaped flowers all over everything.

The beds were liberally spattered with clumps of blue Anchusa which Gramps said was a "pernicious weed and got everywhere", but it looked good in the bigger vases along with Grannie's favourite "aeroplane flower", a strange, yellow-eyed purple bloom with long pointed leaves sticking out down the stem.

There were lines of sweetpeas to cut in summer, and on the whole length of the path beneath the drawing room windows there grew a wide border of Mrs Sinkins, a white garden pink, which sent up great waves of perfume in the sunshine, and whose scent filled the drawing room on summer days. Mrs Sinkins were a "must" for the smaller vases but orange blossom, lilies, geums, hydrangea all came indoors at one time or another.

From June on, roses, roses, roses, of every colour, growing up the house, over arches, standard and bush, and even in parts of the vegetable garden where Gramps had rooted cuttings of such dramatic specimens as the scarlet American Pillar. Cut by the basketful they appeared not only downstairs but in bowls in every bedroom.

Autumn and the scene changed. Blue and purple Michaelmas daisies set off the myriad colours of the dahlias and then the chrysanthemums took over, russet, yellow, pink, they filled the rooms with their distinctive scent until Christmas.

Our flower harvest complete, it was back to the dining room for the careful arranging and transport of the refurbished containers to their usual places round the house.

Grannie loved flowers so at Christmas and on her January birthday relatives and friends showered her with bouquets and pot plants, and these, together with the bowls of hyacinths that had been brought on indoors for the festive season, lent the house the air of a high class florist.

On selected days Grannie took over the polishing of silver or the washing of the most valuable china, all again took place in the dining room with yet more newspaper on the table and two more pairs of gloves!

After whichever discipline had been conducted and the traces of it cleared away, the dining room was left in solitude until the table was laid for luncheon.

This, when I was a small child was a fairly light meal. Gramps always had home-made soup, for the making of which he provided Cook with a variety of vegetables. This was served to him in a special soup bowl, a luridly decorated, pink china monster with two handles, holding well over a pint. Grannie had fish or poultry, never eating red meat after her gall bladder operation.

There would be cold meat or hot fish for everyone else and for dessert, soft fruit in season, the inevitable stewed rhubarb, sometimes gooseberries, apples or pears or either of the latter baked, and a "shape". This was a white blancmange, home made, which Gramps resolutely refused to eat saying it was "a nasty wet thing", while Grannie was as devoted to it as she was to the rhubarb. We had a great deal of the shape, though occasionally there appeared a custard (not out of a packet but made with fresh eggs and milk), rice or tapioca pudding, sometimes the dreaded junket which I loathed but still had to consume without complaint.

The dining room concluded its working day with dinner at seven o'clock for which everyone in my early years changed into evening dress. In later years this was discontinued, although all went up to their respective bedroom and "got ready", which in most cases meant brushing hair, and for the ladies refurbishing any make-up, and in Grannie's case the removal of her stays!

For all, washing hands was in the scant amount of hot water in small brass jugs left on wash hand-stands by the maid.

Dinner consisted of soup, a dish of meat, fowl or game served with the appropriate fresh vegetables from the garden. Grannie was fond of Brussels sprouts but Gramps hated them calling them "waterbags". The pudding could be anything from fruit tart made with home grown fruit and served with thick Jersey cream from the local farm, to French pancakes which, like the junket, I despised but ate without protest, sometimes a boiled sponge pudding served with hot jam. No wine was ever on offer, only a large jug of water from the well.

On Sunday the dining room with its freshly laundered linen, shining glass and silver, played host to the family and any visitors for Sunday dinner served in the middle of the day. A splendid repast ranging from roast beef and Yorkshire pudding to boiled beef and dumplings, a roast leg of best Welsh lamb or loin of pork. Gramps was in his element at the head of the table, wielding the bone handled carving knife and fork and cracking jokes. His favourite, played on unsuspecting guests or sometimes a member of the family whose attention was temporally distracted, took place when a leg of lamb was the main attraction. "Would you like the first cut?" he would enquire innocently of someone. The polite reply came "Yes, please." Whereupon he made the first cut which just left a gap, and laughing hugely would cry "Well, there you are then, you will not get very fat on that!"

Puddings were invariably something with fruit, or an open jam or treacle tart and we finished with cheese and puff biscuits which broke at a touch and scattered crumbs in all directions. My one fear when at the table was that I would knock over a glass of water, and as I was a long armed, restless child and clumsy with it, I often did. What a commotion it caused, as mother leapt up and the maid rushed in. Plates had to be pushed between the linen and the red cloth and between that and the table. Such a mopping and a muttering and I got redder and redder and wished the floor would open and swallow me up.

On Sundays the evening meal was a cold supper which the parlour-maid laid before she and Cook went out for the evening. It was expected of the maids that they would attend service at the little mission church for Evensong, but although they occasionally fulfilled these expectations, they more often went off for a social evening at their respective homes, and who could blame them?

Attending at every meal, Michael the Sealyham sitting up in a resolute begging position on his square rump, paws hanging down and wicked eyes gleaming under his tangled fringe. He chose to position himself between Grannie and Gramps and was fed liberally on tit bits. Gramps gave him all the chop and poultry bones which he crushed up in his great white teeth and swallowed with loud gulpings. Mother was horrified. She was continually telling Gramps that one day a bone would perforate Michael's intestines and he would die in agony. Gramps laughed and pooh-pooed the idea, and strangely enough Michael appeared to bear a charmed life and was never affected by eating such lethal material. In fact he lived to the ripe old age of seventeen years, even surviving jumping out of the bedroom window in pursuit of a passing horseman. Although he did knock himself out for a few minutes, he was as right as rain afterwards and never saw the inside of a veterinary surgery for the whole of his long and sinful life.

The day ended for the dining room with the handing out of the candlesticks by my grandfather as everyone filed up to bed. A prettily skirted silver one with wick scissors and snuffer for Grannie; our candlestick was also silver, plain but with similar accoutrements, while the maids' candlesticks were of plain blue enamel.

When Gramps had seen everyone safely upstairs he repaired to the drawing room to listen to the nine o'clock news on the wireless. This done, in summer he closed the dining room shutters, in winter put out the Aladdin lamp and, taking up his outsize copper candlestick, he too, went up to bed.

In autumn the two logs in the grate fell apart with a dying shower of sparks and smouldered into blackness by the time the Grandfather clock struck the midnight hour.

# CHAPTER
# SIX

# Comings and Goings

Arrivals, departures and trips long or short, the dining room was the starting point for all expeditions to and from the outside world. Here we all assembled whether to go for the afternoon walk with Grannie and Michael, the trips to church or shopping, to catch the bus to Reading, for holidays or just when we were leaving Foxhill for the time being.

Visiting relations were ushered first to the dining room for welcome and at the end of their stay gathered there for farewells. When it came to all these comings and goings, all the threads were held by Mr Smith.

Mr Smith had been a gentleman's gentleman. Rumour had it he had worked for the "best" people and that when his "last gentleman" died (more rumours that this had been no lesser personage than a Duke), Mr Smith was left a legacy that enabled him to buy for his wife and himself a small and comfortable cottage. He acquired a spanking navy blue taxi cab with bright brass lamps, navy leather upholstery, navy silk blinds with a fringe and tassels and a speaking tube covered in the same navy silk finished with a polished wooden plug, and set himself up in business.

The village was some eight miles from Reading, a prodigious distance at that time with an infrequent bus service. Few even of the better off people in the larger houses kept a car, so Mr Smith rapidly became a village institution.

A spare man of military bearing (another rumour was that he had been batman to one of his gentlemen in the Great War) and medium height with receding, short, dark hair just greying at the temples, a good jaw, level blue eyes always with the hint of a smile and a small, trim moustache above a firm mouth. He was friendly without being familiar and civil without servility, and he was genuinely interested in his large clientele, all of whom looked on him as a friend.

Mr Smith was frequently in demand for all our various excursions, my grandparents being without their own transport. While Gramps always took the bus which he caught at the stop opposite the Rising Sun at the top of our road, Grannie's monthly shopping trips to Reading, or visits to dentist, oculist or chiropodist (my grandmother took enormous care of her person), were made in Mr Smith's taxi.

Mr Smith was always on time; if he was ordered for ten thirty the blue taxi would draw up at exactly that hour. Out would get Mr Smith clad in a neat, clerical grey suit, white shirt and black tie, wearing his chauffeur's peaked cap and a pair of brown leather gloves.

We would have been assembled in the dining room for at least fifteen minutes before the off, with any impedimenta such as shopping bags or suitcases depending on the nature of the trip placed in a strategic heap in front of the window.

Mr Smith came briskly up the steps to where Gramps would be at the door, and we would be shepherded down the path under the pergola and handed into the vehicle with great ceremony and a fawn lap robe tucked round our knees.

There was the usual exchange of pleasantries, Grannie enquiring for Mrs Smith, and Mr Smith asking after various members of the family whom he had come to know over his many years of visiting the house.

In those days Reading was a quiet market town, known principally for Suttons Seeds and Huntley and Palmers biscuits. In the main street it was possible for Mr Smith to drive his taxi from shop to shop and wait outside while Grannie made her purchases, and he would be smartly on hand to take them from whichever deferential assistant carried them to the pavement.

The first stop was Baylis the grocers, where the manager in pristine white coat came from behind the counter to greet one of his good customers. A chair was placed on which Grannie seated herself, and then I was invited to inspect the biscuits through the glass framed tops of the tins that lined the outside of the mahogany counter and choose one, usually a Garibaldi known as "squashed flies".

The next stop was Colebrooks the fish and game merchant, usually just to pay the bill, compliment the manager on some order recently received or to place an order for fish to be delivered.

51

The third call was Boots Lending Library as my grandparents were members and my mother and I were junior members. Miss Rendell was the head librarian, a tall, well upholstered lady of great tact and charm, but who ruled her little kingdom with a rod of iron, and valued each and everyone of her clients. Nothing was too much trouble and no book too unknown to be ordered and procured from somewhere within a few days.

Once Mr Smith had stowed the library books in the car he was free to go to lunch or do whatever he pleased, as from Boots we walked along to Heelas, a very high-class department store. Here we visited the department where all the knitting wools and embroidery silks, needles, pins, cottons and the rest of the haberdashery was sold. As a small girl it was my favourite stop, not because I had any interest in needlecraft, much to the sorrow of Grannie and Mother, but because the money Grannie paid to the assistant behind the counter was screwed into those little wooden containers and sent spinning round the shop on rails at the pull of a handle.

Sometimes we visited the hat department when Grannie would choose a new brown straw for summer or felt for winter. These hats were always the same and I did wonder why she bothered to buy any more when her hat drawer contained their exact replicas. Sometimes she had a new dress choosing several which we took "on approval" to be tried on in the privacy of her own home, the unchosen ones being returned to the shop.

Grannie treated us to lunch in the store's well appointed restaurant where the waitresses were all rather old having been there since they left school. They knew all their "regulars" and, although rather slow, the service was all that could be desired.

Grannie knew all of them and they all knew her, and whichever came to serve us would say to her, "I expect it will be a nice lemon sole, won't it, madam?" They were always correct.

Mr Smith, who had been told to be on stand-by at two o'clock, was of course waiting outside the store ready to take the parcels from the assistant and then it was sedately back to Foxhill for Grannie to have a short rest before tea.

When my grandparents went on their annual two weeks holiday to Wales each summer, John came in to help Mr Smith out with all the impedimenta. The trunk, a suitcase, Gramps's dressing case, Grannie's dressing case and hat box, and a bundle of walking sticks, umbrellas, sunshades and rugs were the least the taxi was expected to hold.

Gramps, clad in his second best brown suit and his bowler hat, and Grannie in one of her long, brown dresses, a travelling coat, one of the famous hats perched square on her head and fastened with hat pins and a veil, were at last eased into the taxi and mother and I fitted in somehow.

"Now we'll soon have you on that train," Mr Smith would exclaim as he carefully closed the door.

As a child I found this a most exciting occasion. While the porters and Mr Smith were settling the luggage on a trolley, my grandfather purchased the tickets and Grannie gave me three pennies to put in the machine to get the platform tickets for mother, myself and of course, Mr Smith: no holiday could start unless his reassuring figure was present and the old people could steam away content in the knowledge that he would convey us safely back to Foxhill.

There were two other machines on Platform 1, a penny in the first delivered a delicious thin bar of Nestlé's chocolate, while the other, for the same price, printed your name on a piece of tin as long as you pressed the correct buttons. I used to go home with both.

When the train came in snorting and belching steam, my grandfather would go purposefully up to the cab and shake hands with the driver bidding him take good care on the journey. Gramps took seats in the first coach as he had an idea that if there was a crash you would be safer there than anywhere else on the train. I am not sure who gave him this idea.

At last the luggage was stowed in the guard's van, the holiday makers seated with their newspapers, library books and lunch basket, the guard blew a shrill whistle, waved his green flag, and with a great roaring and billowing of smoke the train pulled out of the station and we could make our way home in the comfort of Mr Smith's taxi.

After Christmas one year we went to stay at Foxhill for several months. It was during the two years I was attending a small dame's school for girls on Caversham

Heights. No Mr Smith for me, I had to rise early and catch the bus to Reading.

The dining room was freezing cold at seven thirty as the two logs, although lighting with a fine crackle and shower of pine sparks, soon subsided into their usual dull slumber as this wood will unless constantly fortified.

My insides in a knot, I never could choke down any breakfast although both mother and the parlour-maid, vastly concerned for my health and well being, tried in vain to get me to eat anything from porridge to bacon and eggs; the most I ever managed was a few nibbles at a banana. I was going through an awkward stage at about thirteen and must have been suffering some nervous tension, possibly a delayed reaction to the sudden death of my father some thirteen months earlier. That sort of thing was not recognised in children at that time, and if I had one of my "funny" turns I was told to pull myself together and not be silly.

I was always sent off much too early and stood shivering on the bus stop that had no shelter except the Major's high wooden wall with the wild hedge growing over the top. Often fifteen minutes in the rain or cold, later in hot sun, hating the idea of the trip and once on the bus sitting with clenched fingers and teeth and longing for the day to end. It was not that I disliked school, on the contrary I was very happy there; it was, I suppose, just the idea of leaving the safety of Foxhill.

At one time the bus terminus was in St Mary's Butts where in the Middle Ages archers practised with the long bow. Then the terminus was moved to the station yard where I had to change buses for the one for the Heights. The station yard in those days had a large meadow on the far side and here Bertram Mills Circus came each year and pitched their big top.

How thankful I was each afternoon to climb into the bus at the station, eagerly waiting for the conductor to pull the bell and signal my return trip home.

Through the familiar streets of the old town, then to the Butts and into the Bath Road, down past the Old Kennels where once the foxhounds were kept and there was a pub called The World's End. Left into the winding road that led through little hamlets with their familiar inn signs, the Hatch Gate, the White Swan, the Cunning Man, the latter a favourite as the inn sign portrayed a grinning face peering through a thicket of green leaves. Past the Mother church with its spreading graveyard where my old people now lie. Through the village proper and up the steep winding hill to the Common, the way signposted by the pointing fingers of three tall Redwood trees on the estate of Mr Figgis who lived in solitary splendour with an old housekeeper to minister to his wants.

How I raced down the road from the Rising Sun, pausing only to pop the seeds of the yellow shrub that hung over Mr King's fence, and then in at the white gate with someone always watching for my return and holding open the big green door, then into the dining room where Michael would jump about and bark for joy and there was a splendid tea waiting for me.

# CHAPTER
# SEVEN

# Down the Steps to the Drawing Room

The drawing room was strictly Grannie's domain. She loved light and air and when the room was planned requested windows in all three outside walls as well as French windows to the garden.

The door into the drawing room was set in the top right hand wall if you viewed the room from the end, and it faced the window in the south wall under which was set Grannie's rosewood writing table.

To the right of the door, hanging from a picture rail set high on the wall, was an immense mirror in an ornate gold frame, all acanthus leaves and cabbage roses. Under this stood a highly polished table, kept upright on a pedestal from which several curved feet inlaid with brass sprouted. This was the silver table and held many cherished pieces handed down through the family or brought back by my grandparents from foreign travels in their younger days.

My favourite piece on the table was a stirrup cup made in the shape of the head of an Arab horse and inscribed "Frankfort on Main. 1868". I christened him

"Ahmed" and loved him dearly. Many, many years later my Uncle G, on one of my visits to him in his old age, produced Ahmed from a cabinet and gave him to me saying "You are the one most interested in horses in this family. You had better have him now, you might not get him when I have gone!" His words were very prophetic, for although I was left a third of his estate when he died, most was whisked off to the sale rooms by a cousin before I had a chance to choose anything to keep.

When he gave me Ahmed, Uncle G gave my mother an inkwell shaped liked the head of an elephant with a tiny monkey sitting between its ears, which had also been an occupant of the silver table.

The maids were not expected to clean any of the silver in this display although they had to dust it daily. Once a month we had a silver morning. The inevitable roll of newspaper was spread over the dining room table and Grannie donned an old pair of chamois leather gloves, out came the Goddards plate powder and a saucer to mix it in, sundry polishers and soft dusters, and she set to work, whoever was staying at the time being delegated to assist.

One night when I was about eleven, we were woken by a muffled crash in the middle of the night. My mother, who disliked loud noises in the extreme, was convinced it was thunder and stuck her head under her pillow. However in the morning there came a great wail from the drawing room which lay beneath our bedroom, and we grabbed dressing-gowns and rushed down to find the parlour-maid in tears.

The huge mirror had detached itself from its moorings in the night and crashed down in the silver table.

Strangely neither the mirror itself nor any of the silver was damaged, although the table suffered a few scratches and the gold leaves and roses took a battering.

The mirror was so large that it reflected all that was going on in the room, and on winter evenings when the Aladdin lamp shed its dubious glow, all sorts of shadows seemed to move, and I imagined I could see strange shapes in the corners of the room, or pale faces peering over my shoulder.

In summer the mirror was a joy because it reflected all the many bowls of flowers my grandmother loved to have around her and great was the rejoicing when the mirror was re-hung, unbroken and in its accustomed position.

The corner between Grannie's desk and the silver display was home to a spindly legged table topped by a tall vase in which a bunch of Pampas grass lived permanently, although I think it possibly got a yearly renewal from the huge clump growing on the side lawn.

There was a pretty three sided cupboard hanging in the corner of the wall on the opposite side and this contained delicate pieces of china and a wonderful collection of small china animals, with which I was allowed to play when I had been very good. They were quite charming and I was always very careful of them, afraid I should break one and never again be allowed to play with them. I often wonder what became of them.

On the north wall, beyond the door, was the first of two china cabinets the other sited beyond the window. Glass fronted, they contained valuable tea sets which to my knowledge were never used. One was Crown Derby which Uncle G inherited; this I know because once when visiting him, I had to go to the cellar to retrieve some pictures for him and saw this prized china on a shelf; it was covered in coal dust. My mother begged him to bring it upstairs and put it in one of his cabinets, but he said it would do very well where it was. No doubt it fetched a good price when the house and contents were sold on his death at the great age of 96.

The first of Grannie's cabinets housed the "Nantgarw plate" which came to my mother and had to be sold to pay the bills in one of our many penniless moments.

On top of this cabinet, several china ornaments surrounded a Dutch clock, known in the family as "the Ormolu" though whether it was made of this material is a moot point. It was a large square piece with a sort of pagoda top, a plain white face with large hands and a deep compelling voice which contrasted with the Dresden clock on the mantelpiece, who, from its covering of pale blue and pink flowers and fruit, issued forth its challenge in a sweet silvery tone like the sound of a waterfall.

My mother inherited the Dresden clock which sang as sweetly as it had for my grandmother, that is until the advent of the Singing Bird. This was a canary that belonged to my aunt. The creature suffered from claustrophobia (she said) so it lived loose in her flat and would perch on the parrot's cage. The parrot took against this invasion of its space and bit several toes off the canary, who in consequence, to save its remaining toes, was brought round as a gift for my mother.

The Singing Bird, left free to fly round our sitting room, took up residence on top of the Dresden clock but what it deposited down the back of the clock somehow got inside and jammed up the works, so the clock took umbrage and has refused to go ever since.

However, in Grannie's drawing room the Dresden clock kept exemplary time, always being a couple of seconds ahead of the Ormolu which was known to be on the slow side. On each end of the mantelpiece a pair of scantily dressed Dresden ladies in reclining positions held sway, along with two pretty French vases, one filled with the inevitable paper spills.

Above the mantelpiece hung the most lovely watercolour of a shaggy dog sitting on a heather-clad hillside with a dead rabbit at its feet. The painting was so lifelike that you expected the dog to bark. Gramps had purchased this picture at an auction sale in the early 1900s, and this came to us when the house was sold up. It was far too large to be accommodated on any wall in any of the variety of dwellings in which we resided over the years, and that too was sadly sold.

The fireplace, alas, did not boast an open fire, but instead a strange, many faceted, pale blue stove of some ceramic material. It burned anthracite and gave off enough fumes to put a whole village to sleep. On winter evenings when I was old enough to stay up for dinner, I can remember watching my grandmother fighting to stay awake over a game of Patience, mother nodding over her knitting and Gramps far away in dreamland, his detective novel on his chest, while I could feel my eyelids shutting against my will. Why the whole family was not wiped out I cannot imagine.

In winter Grannie's sofa was set, end-on, to the fireplace, with Gramps's big armchair opposite. Beside his chair was a small, black japanned table decorated with colourful flowers. On this a large glass ashtray, his pipe, matches and "baccy" pouch, his library book, the current copy of the *Financial Times* and a pair of wire framed magnifying glasses he had purchased for 6d from Woolworths (never in his life did he visit an oculist), and a small, oval topped wireless set with a fretwork front.

The wireless was strictly Gramps's affair, no-one else would dare have touched it. It was a pretty primitive device and the sound left a great deal to be desired. It had been given to him and installed by Cousin Raymond who had gone in for this new manner of communication in a big way and had a house full of sets and yards of wires hanging in festoons over which everyone tripped.

Only certain programmes were ever switched on. One was the six o'clock news, mainly because at the end the racing results were given. Gramps was an inveterate gambler on the gee-gees, albeit for minor stakes at that time. So he sat with the *Daily Telegraph* folded at the racing page, pencil poised, while I hung over the back of his chair eager to give assistance in spotting the horses' names as they were read out over the air waves, rejoicing with him with a silent hug when he got a winner.

Grannie strongly disapproved of her husband's love of racing, which my mother inherited, although when with Grannie she kept awfully quiet about it, but I was openly on Gramps's side and the daily racing results were as much fun for me as for him especially as we had to operate under Grannie's keen eye.

Set in the south wall behind Gramps's chair were the French windows, always open in summer so the glorious scents of the old fashioned flowers in the beds across the gravelled path could waft into the room, especially the scent of the Mrs Sinkins pinks, which, when encountered today, can still transport me back to Foxhill. In winter the French windows were covered with long, heavy curtains to minimise the draught. The end wall was set with a large window overlooking the side lawn where a thick privet hedge divided it from the hay meadow. In front of this window stood a chaise longue. This was upholstered in shiny, black rexine and stuffed so tightly with horsehair that it was not only slippery but as hard as iron to sit on. The head and back were of polished wood, intricately carved; this meant that to lean back was to end up with a deep pattern engraved on your shoulders.

To minimise the discomfort to whoever was unwise enough to occupy it, the chaise longue was garnished with two round, wine coloured silk cushions, but as they had buttons skewered through their middles and appeared to have been stuffed with rocks, they were not much help. It was on this uncomfortable object that my elder cousin would drape himself placing a cologne scented handkerchief over his face and complain of one of his dreadful headaches, and this at 18 years of age!

Behind the chaise longue were three plant holders, oblong, tin lined and standing on odd shaped bamboo legs. These contained pots of aspidistras and maidenhair ferns and smelt rather horrid. The whole thing was set off by larger than life-sized white marble busts of great grandfather and great-great grandfather that stood on either side of the window.

The grandfathers were a source of delight at spring cleaning time, as I was allowed to stand on a chair and wash them with hot, soapy water, dislodging any dust in the crevices of their eyes and whiskers with someone's discarded toothbrush and shoving cones of wet cotton wool up their aristocratic nostrils. It was a most satisfying exercise and the only time I felt I had got the better of adults!

In summer Grannie's sofa was pulled over to rest under the north window, the second china cabinet standing between it and great grandfather's bust. This cabinet contained the Minton china but I am not sure what happened to this either. Michael found the placing of the sofa to his liking. His sentinel's post was the chaise longue, standing on the shiny surface with his shaggy hind legs close together and his front paws gripping the carved back. He could just see over the privet hedge enough to discern anyone coming down the road.

Any human or animal that dared to approach the house was a signal for uproarious barking, and he leapt from his perch, jumped up on Grannie's sofa, ran along the back, down the end and roared off over the top of her and, if the door was open, hurtled through the dining room to the study where the window seat awaited him and he could get a real sight of the enemy and hurl abuse at them.

It did not matter to Michael that Grannie was ensconced on the sofa, he just took her in his stride, and after his departure she would brush down her skirt, rescue her knitting or sewing and remark "What a wretched dog he is!"

Precisely at eleven o'clock every morning the parlour-maid brought Grannie a cup of Horlicks or Sanatogen, and two biscuits, one for her and one for "that wretched dog" who, for all his dreadful habits, both she and Gramps loved dearly.

Grannie took her refreshment at her desk where she would be busy answering letters; she was a prodigious letter writer and kept in touch with numberless relations on both sides of the family. At that time too she would add to her Boots Library list from the Books Page in the *Telegraph*, put out settlement for tradesmen's accounts, and make lists of friends or acquaintances who (a) had to be called upon, (b) had to be invited for some meal or (c) were to come and stay.

Grannie's mother was French and, like so many of that race, my grandmother was an excellent organiser in the home. Particular and persistent, she was a great trainer of young girls coming into service, although Grannie, apart from the lamps, silver cleaning and china washing, had never done any housework herself. Nor had she ever in her lifetime had to cook anything, except once.

She used to tell the story of how she and Gramps were on their honeymoon in the family yacht and it was moored off the Algerian coast. Being unable to go ashore owing to the sudden dangers to be encountered and thinking that a young bride should know something of cooking, she asked the ship's cook to attend her, and when he did so, requested that he teach her some culinary skills. He suggested she make a roly poly pudding which she did, but overdid the ingredients so that when she rolled the suet crust round the jam came up with a pudding so long it would not fit into any of the pots! That was the end of the culinary effort, and as far as I am aware, she never tried cooking again for the whole of her 95 years!

The drawing room came very much alive at four o'clock: the recognised tea time. Gramps would come in from the garden, attended by me, and we would find Grannie and my mother sitting waiting for us. The trolley from outside the door had been wheeled to Grannie's side and was laid with one of the hand embroidered cloths, and held the beautiful silver tea set that had been a wedding present, the squat teapot chased with a pattern of flowers with the delicate rose on the lid and matching jug with wide lip and a large sugar bowl filled with lump sugar and attended by silver tongs.

There was a silver kettle singing over a small flame from a small glass container of methylated spirit with a lighted wick in it, and a set of fragile bone china cups and saucers. Between Gramps's chair and the tea trolley, a drop sided table had been opened and also boasted an embroidered cloth. This was set with plates of wafer thin bread and butter, sandwiches in a similar vein, in summer usually home grown cucumber, while in winter a dish of toasted muffins or crumpets hiding under a round silver cover would be keeping warm on top of the stove.

A three tiered cake stand completed the ensemble, and inevitably held a jam sponge on the top shelf and a sultana cake on the second, unless the vicar was expected when this delicacy was replaced by a seed cake though for what reason I never found out. I certainly do not think the vicar was addicted to seed cake as he had a full set of ill fitting dentures, and Gramps and I used to wink in a conspiratorial manner as the agitated man of the cloth tried to keep his eyes from watering when a recalcitrant seed got under his plate.

On the bottom shelf, was a plate of home made shortbread and Michael had to be watched carefully as he was a dab hand at filching a biscuit when no-one was watching, and if they were, he simply sat up and begged and got one anyway.

If some of the family were staying, tea was a very jolly affair, especially if Aunt Lovey was one of the party for she was guaranteed to bring fun wherever she went. With her outsize sense of the ridiculous she soon had everyone laughing, even my staid grandmother joining in.

In winter all were drawn to the jig-saw puzzle set up on a side table. Consisting of about 1000 pieces and usually without a picture to follow, it kept everyone amused at odd moments, trying to work out what the picture represented and be able to select pieces to help complete it. Some puzzles took several weeks and had a whole clutch of people involved in their completion. There was always great competition to put in the final piece.

My most abiding memory of Grannie in her drawing room is of the beautiful needlework she accomplished. Educated in a French convent, she was expert on the lace pillow, she crocheted lace and babies' jackets and shawls. Her knitting looked as if it was untouched by human hands; she made all Gramps's long stockings, knitting quickly on four slim, steel needles, and knitted his favourite sleeveless pullovers as well as the yellow roll necks favoured by my cousins and myself for several years.

Grannie's embroidery was of the finest and in the early 1930s she embarked on an enormous bed spread in cream linen which was covered in a design of roses from one side to the other and set out to be worked in cross-stitch. Grannie would set aside all other work for one hour each day to apply herself to this task, and every member of the family, male and female, had to put a few stitches in the pattern. The whole took several years to complete and to finish it off she crocheted a six inch deep border of lace with a rose motif to frame it. This historic masterpiece survives in the ownership of my daughter.

Although my step-sister had been an apt pupil at Grannie's knee, I was a sad disappointment. However, with Grannie's usual persistence and my mother's help, I was taught to embroider, knit and crochet, but I was always far happier outside with the animals and helping in the garden.

Apart from all the knitting and needlework she did for family and friends, Grannie was a tireless worker for charity, embroidering altar cloths for the church, knitting children's jumpers and dolls' clothes for the village bazaars and being a great supporter of Agnes Weston's Homes for Sailors, several times a year sending parcels of immaculately knitted navy jerseys and many pairs of sea boot stockings. She also knitted innumerable pairs of operation stockings for the hospital.

Whenever you went into the drawing room Grannie's busy fingers would be at work, only in the early evening did she rest and play Patience, and on Sunday read a book.

One great ritual of the drawing room was "the chocolates". When people become older few knew what to give them as presents so along with the flowers came boxes of chocolates. These were locked in the second drawer down on the left side of her writing table and each afternoon, after luncheon, she would solemnly unlock the drawer, take out a box and allow everyone just one chocolate. The box was then locked away till the next day. My mother, who loved chocolate, was not the only one hoping for a few more, but Grannie

**69**

considered one chocolate a day a sufficiency for anyone.

This parsimony meant that there were always several boxes of chocolates that were of great age, and many that were handed round had white spotted contents, but none were wasted and none of us were any the worse for eating them! Aunt Lovey used to expostulate with her mother; she was the only one with enough courage to tackle that determined lady, and suggest that we ate up at least one box, earning the rebuke "Really, Lovey, how can you be so greedy!" as if my aunt was still 12 years old and not in her fifties!

So many memories of that gracious room that always smelled of wax polish, chintz and flowers, with just a hint of Gramps's fragrant tobacco. A happy room with just one sad memory.

One afternoon in the spring of 1931 the shrill voice of the telephone broke the calm of the day. Why I was in the drawing room at three o'clock in the afternoon I have no idea, I was usually in the garden or paddock or roaming about the common or woods, but I was there when mother went through to answer the call and I trotted after her. I saw the agonised look on her expression as she listened to the voice on the other end, saw her face whiten and she cried out in a strange voice, 'Oh no! Oh my God, no!'

I can clearly remember running through the dining room and into the drawing room where my grandmother stood motionless, sensing something was wrong. I flung myself into her arms and cried out, "Something has happened to Daddy, I know it has!"

Grannie was not a demonstrative woman. Corseted from bust to buttocks and immaculately gowned and regal in her carriage, she was not a person with which to take liberties, although her gentle hands could soothe the most fractious baby. But that day she held me against her and smoothed my hair. We said nothing but we both knew what had happened.

When I was very little I played in the summer sunshine on the steps outside the French windows with my stuffed animals and teddies. When we arrived to stay after a tiring journey, a small table for tea was set for me by the window, with a new laid egg and bread and butter as a special treat.

The day for the drawing room drew to a close at nine fifteen precisely. At ten to nine Grannie rose from her sofa and so did we all, and Gramps would kiss us all good night and usher us up to the dining room to be issued with our candlesticks if the nights were dark. It used to give Aunt L the giggles, a crowd of grown people being sent up to bed at nine o'clock each night, but that was the rule.

When we were gone, the old man settled down to hear the nine o'clock news and smoke a last pipe and at nine fifteen he followed the family up to rest.

# CHAPTER
# EIGHT

# Family Gatherings

There were great family gatherings at Foxhill, such as the party for Gramps's 90th birthday, although my poor mother was on the verge of rheumatic fever and spent most of the day wrapped in a shawl huddled over the two logs in the dining room, while relations circulated and chatted and ate lunch and tea.

The house got very crowded during the day and when the crush was at its height in the dining room, Aunt L got shut behind the door. Everyone was enquiring where she had got to, and at last her piteous wails were heard over the hubbub, and the hefty second-cousin-once-removed who was leaning on the door shifted his weight and she was discovered amid much hilarity.

Aunt Mabel, Uncle G's formidable wife and a keen horticulturist, after her walk down the vegetable garden, informed Gramps that her broad beans were far more advanced than his and nearly caused another family feud, the last one having ended a few years beforehand, mother and Aunt M only just on speaking terms.

The story handed down the family went like this. Uncle G married his first cousin Mabel on the rebound when he was jilted by the girl he adored. Mabel, who had carried a torch for her handsome cousin from childhood, had only been waiting for a chance and seized him when his defences were down.

Aunt Mabel was a large uncomfortable-looking woman, always appearing to have been bundled into her clothes, florid of face and with masses of white hair piled up inside a hairnet. Christened Helen Mabel Sophanisba which unfortunately gave her the initials HMS, Aunt L used to say no-one was better named as Aunt Mabel did not so much walk as forge along rather like a battleship at half speed.

Anyway, mother, who disliked her cousin Mabel intensely, went to her beloved brother's wedding and wept copiously through the entire service. Outside the church following the nuptials, the father of the bride surveying his tear-stained niece, enquired, "Why are you crying, Gwenllian?" My mother, sobbing piteously replied "You would cry too if your brother was marrying such an awful woman!" This honest answer caused a rift that took several decades to heal!

When visiting Foxhill Aunt Mabel used to stump round the drawing room peering into all the cabinets and examining the silver on the table, and after she had gone Aunt Lovey would say tartly to my mother "I see Mabel is keeping an eye on the pieces she hopes to get!"

Mother's chief gripe about her sister-in-law seemed to be that when she was a girl, Mabel and her sister Helen ate mutton chops and steak for breakfast! Aunt

M was still a prodigious eater, although she only got bacon and eggs for breakfast at Foxhill, but when at dinner never ceased to tell everyone that she had a small appetite. The fact that she got through a generous first helping and then when asked, if she would like more, would giggle like a girl and say to Gramps, "Well, just a little, please, Uncle Frank" and soon be consuming another two hefty slices of meat, belied her statement.

Great Uncle Charlie was Grannie's brother and everyone adored him. I can see his tall, handsome figure standing in the drawing room, gold watch in hand, making it chime to please me when I was very young.

Grannie and Great Uncle Charlie had lost their mother when they were small children, and had been brought up by their grandparents as their father married again. Their grandfather was C. B. Vignoles, celebrated soldier and Civil Engineer. His second wife was a handsome Portuguese lady who spoke not one word of English. She bore him eleven more children of whom five brothers, all civil engineers, went off to build the railroads in South America where they all married Spanish or Portuguese beauties and sired innumerable gorgeous offspring.

The brothers died one by one of TB, but every few years wealthy and glamorous descendants would come to England and visit their relation at Foxhill.

I chiefly remember them for the chocolates they brought as gifts. Huge, square, polished wooden boxes, several inches in depth, and with little brass hinges and clasps. Opened, they revealed many satin lined compartments in each one of which rested a magnificent chocolate of great size.

We were each allowed to select one, but of course, when the visitors had departed, Grannie gathered up all our chocolates, wrapped them in tissue paper and consigned them to the chocolate drawer. Each mouth-watering beauty was later cut up into several pieces, the glorious fillings oozing out, and we were allowed, yes, one piece each a day!

Grannie's step-sisters and the step-brother who stayed in England were frequent visitors. The great aunts Ethel, Alice and Lily and Great Uncle Ernest lived not far distant in the Thames Valley, variously at Pangbourne and Goring. Our favourite was Aunt Ethel, who had remained unmarried. She was very like Grannie in looks and character, with great dignity and charm and possessed of infinite patience and kindness.

Aunt Alice was tall and forbidding. She loved my step-sister and was a very good friend to her, but she was not too keen on me, regarding me as a harum-scarum tomboy, and frequently lecturing my mother on the necessity of making me more civilised and lady-like and therefore more acceptable to her.

For my part I disliked Aunt Alice fiercely and when she came to visit I bolted for the kitchen, begging Cook to hide me under the voluminous folds of the red cloth which, every afternoon, was slung over the kitchen table. Inevitably I was found by my mother, dragged out and given a severe talking to, brushed down and taken off to attend the tea party in the drawing room.

Mother could never understand my aversion to Great Aunt Alice, with whom she had always had a fond relationship, and she often told me tales of when Great Uncle Gordon Lennox was alive how she attended the wonderful house parties on their large estate at Tardebigg where she and her brother and sister enjoyed themselves enormously. Perhaps after her handsome husband died Aunt Alice changed.

Great Aunt Lily was small and pushy and also a widow. She was quite a jolly, friendly soul and I tolerated her to a certain extent. She was inclined to be bossy which annoyed Gramps who, when an impending visit was announced, hastily arranged a trip to Reading on urgent business!

Great Uncle Ernest was a bachelor, very tall, willowy, handsome but rather effeminate. He was also very clever, a brilliant electrical engineer, and rich, but spoken of in hushed tones as being mean. He was the senior partner in the firm of Evershed and Vignoles and when not attending to business was a very keen photographer and possibly one of the first people to own his own ciné camera. He did not like children much, so conversed little, but he was clued up enough to know that at the end of a visit it was the done thing to press a welcome half crown into the hand of any great niece or nephew present when he left at the end of a visit.

The great occasion in the late 1930s was that of my grandparents' Diamond Wedding. The village was agog, as the post mistress had actually written out the telegram of congratulation from the King and Queen

**76**

and an awe struck telegraph boy had delivered it and received a welcome shilling from Gramps.

Uncle G and Aunt Mabel were staying in the house and Aunt Lovey and my cousins arrived from London by car in time for breakfast, and the house was overflowing by the time the buffet lunch was announced.

Great Uncle Ernest had brought his ciné camera; not only that, the film was to record the occasion in colour. After the repast and the cutting of the magnificent cake, recorded on film, we all went into the bright April sunshine where the camera man insisted the ladies carry bright coloured flowers or wear them in their hair. We were photographed in procession crossing the lawn led by the happy couple.

I was going through an awkward, bolshy, teenage stage at the time (although in those days teenage was not something that was recognised) but I remember being quite unpleasant about having to carry a rose and hold my mother's hand, and I am sure I scowled! I often wonder what happened to that historic film.

# CHAPTER NINE

# The Magic of the Kitchen

The kitchen was a magical place. There was always something going on, calls at the back door from tradesmen, bells ringing, maids scurrying about, Cook baking, peeling, beating. When we were small there was the added thrill of being in almost forbidden territory in case we got in the way of the maids.

At the end of the hall there was a sharp turn, the door to the cellar steps was on the right and that into the back porch on the left, the kitchen door was straight ahead.

High on the left hand wall, just inside the kitchen door, was a panel with a row of bells which were used to summon the maids to any room in the house, each bearing a number. I do not remember any of them working and they seemed to remain as a reminder of grander days.

I suppose the kitchen was, by the standards of the day, on the small side. There was a large sash window in the south wall with a window seat underneath. This boasted two rather worn patchwork cushions and usually a tidy pile of the maids' reading matter, weekly magazines such as "*Red Star*" and "*Poppy*" and romances from the penny library.

The porcelain sink with its well scrubbed wooden draining board was on the wall behind the door. The cupboard underneath held cleaning appliances and two washing up bowls, a papier mâché one in which all the silver and glass was washed, and an enamel one for the crockery, while the pots and pans went into the sink.

Owing to the scarcity of hot water the glass and silver were washed up first and the used water tipped into the enamel bowl for the china, and from there the water went into the sink to be topped up with a boiling kettle for the pots and pans. Very little hot water ever got used from the tap in the kitchen; it was so scarce it had to be saved for the bathroom.

The hand pump was fixed to the north wall and three times a day the water had to be pumped up from the well into the tanks in the attic that serviced the kitchen and bathroom. This operation was done at nine, noon and five by John. The rhythmical thump-thump, thump-thump, thump-thump, as the handle was energetically worked back and forth could be heard throughout the house.

It was considered wise by those who had reason to visit the kitchen not to do so during this ritual, as these were the days before bathrooms in every cottage and universal bathing by the population at large, and certainly before the days of antiperspirants. John, coming in already hot from his labours in the garden, and then lustily working the pump for ten or fifteen minutes, made the kitchen very odorous!

The water, heavily impregnated with iron, came from a well outside the back door, and all the water to drink, wash up or bath in, had a rusty shade. The well was said to be "bottomless". It certainly never ran dry during my grandparents' tenure at Foxhill and we had some very dry summers.

The well gave my rather vivid imagination much scope, I dreamed up all sorts of wonderful yarns about it and peopled it with strange inhabitants. As far as I know the only dwellers in the well were large green frogs and a few immense beige coloured slugs, which I watched with fascination when the well cover was removed every so often by Gramps and John for a ritual inspection, to check the water level.

No official ever came to check the water quality as they would today, but whatever it contained, we all seemed remarkably healthy. All of us, apart from my mother who considered water only useful to wash in, drank the well water and I for one loved its brackish irony taste.

Next to the hand pump stood the big dresser, with its deep drawers that always seemed to be able to supply any item needed by a member of the staff or the family. The shelves displayed the willow-patterned service in daily use, from the hooks hung the large, breakfast cups.

On the top shelf, cake and biscuit tins, no doubt put up high out of temptation's way, Cook's large brown tea pot, a line of six white egg cups each hand-painted with a different breed of fowl, and an egg timer.

Mrs Beeton's *"Book of Household Management"* and several other cookery books, including one entitled *"Jams and Preserves"*, and two smaller volumes *"Hay Box Cookery"* and *"Light Dishes for Invalids"*, were neatly stacked at the back.

The cupboards underneath were full of bowls and dishes, jelly moulds, a pestle and mortar, cheese grater, hair and wire sieves, a cast-iron mincer that screwed to the kitchen table, and other useful objects.

In a cupboard set up an the same wall were the "dry goods". This was known as the "store cupboard" and was securely locked, the key being kept on Grannie's key ring. It was not considered frugal for the cook to have control of the ingredients for cooking (cooks could be extravagant, and it was not unknown in some houses for the cook to actually sell some of her employer's groceries to others!).

My grandmother always said "Never put temptation in people's way", so the store cupboard, like the chocolate drawer, was kept locked!

Under the store cupboard another larger cupboard was full of the impedimenta then necessary to run a kitchen successfully, on the top a beautiful set of copper scales with brass weights in which every item used in the cookery was meticulously weighed. Beside this cupboard stood the bread crock with a wooden lid.

On the wall facing the door was "the kitchener", a monstrous, black, cast-iron stove kept clean and bright by the constant application of much black lead and elbow grease, its steel knobs and handles brightly burnished.

It did not, of course, stay in overnight, so each morning the cook had to be up very early to get it started with the sticks and coal brought in and stacked in the porch by John, as there would be no water for the household's early tea until the stove was hot enough to boil the kettle, nor indeed the small amount of hot water for the baths.

Should the wind be in the wrong direction the stove could prove almost impossible to light, and once it did catch would puff huge breaths of acrid smoke into the kitchen through its teeth, as I liked to think of the bars that held in the bright coals when it was burning happily.

Every week the kitchener had to have its flues cleaned, an even earlier start for Cook, and the whole house would be awakened by the banging and rattling as she forced the brush up and down the flues.

Every year the chimney needed cleaning, and this was accomplished by the chimney sweep who arrived at around four-thirty in the morning, and so completed his task in time for Cook to lay and light the stove for early tea and to cook breakfast before the family made their appearance.

The sweep made a great deal of mess in those days, and the evening before his arrival to sweep any chimney was spent removing all the pictures and ornaments, and covering everything in dust sheets, while in the kitchen much the same scene prevailed. The day the sweep came was a signal for Grannie to order cold meals so the cook could spend all day cleaning up and getting her domain back to normal.

One spring Gramps decided that the sweep was an unnecessary extravagance and he could quite well do the chimneys himself. He proposed to send John up onto the roof with a small holly bush on either end of which was tied a rope. John would send one end of the rope down the chimney. Gramps would be waiting by the hearth and when he caught the end he could haul the bush down the chimney and John on the other end could haul it back again and they would continue in this fashion until the prickly leaves of the holly had loosened all the soot and sent it down into the room.

My grandmother was horrified at the thought of the mess it would make, and utterly forbade the exercise, much to the disappointment of the two would-be sweeps and myself, who foresaw great fun in the whole enterprise. So Gramps, on a Saturday trip to Reading market, invested in a device called "The Imp, guaranteed to clean any chimney without the aid of a sweep". The instructions were to lay the fire with paper and wood, place the Imp in the middle, and apply a lighted match to the kindling. Perhaps in view of what occurred it should have read "light the blue touch paper and retire immediately"!

Gramps, without telling Grannie, realising that without doubt she would have spoilt his fun, decided to clean the kitchen chimney with the Imp, so one morning, when Cook was laying the fire, he appeared and told her what he intended to do. The cook, who no doubt cast a despairing eye to heaven, demurred not at all. She, like all the maids, we ever had, were used to "the Master's little ways"!

The stove was laid, the Imp placed in the centre of the kindling and a lighted match was applied. It was a good job they both stood back, because Gramps had forgotten one little necessity, he had forgotten to open the flue!

The Imp, igniting perfectly, glowed a brilliant red for a few moments and then went off like a rocket, but unable to get up the chimney blew out the whole of the front of the stove!

The noise, the soot and the smell, brought the entire household to the spot. Gramps, black from head to foot, stood rocking with laughter, it was the best explosion he had caused in a long time and quite eclipsed the last experiment in the study. The cook, black of face and with shaking hands, was throwing her apron over her head and wailing in a banshee-like manner.

John, rushing in from outside, stood gawping, open mouthed. Mother was saying in her most severe voice "Really, Father, what will you do next, you could have blown us all up in our beds!" Grannie just stood speechless, no doubt deciding what she was going to say to the naughty old man when she got him alone.

The parlour-maid was keeping well out of the way in the passage while an elderly cousin who was staying, suddenly realised he was standing open mouthed and that he had forgotten to put his teeth in, hurriedly departed, red faced.

It turned out that Gramps had another Imp which he had intended to use in the drawing room stove. What a good job he practised on the kitchener first!

Permanent fixtures on top of the stove were a large, black kettle, always gently steaming, and the stock pot. The latter was a noxious thing kept in those days, simmering forever on stoves up and down the land. It contained all the odd left overs, bones, bits of meat, vegetables, bacon rinds, bread crusts etc. Filled to the brim with water, it simmered on its merry way emitting a sort of stuffy, sickly odour, and was used as a base for all soups and gravies. Overnight, as the stove expired, it went cold, and in the morning it slowly hotted up once the stove got going. It was Cook's custom to "give it a good boil" once a day, perhaps that is why none of us suffered from ptomaine poisoning!

Either side of the stove were long cupboards built into the wall full to the brim with useful objects. The mantelpiece was covered in a wine coloured material and fastened at the front edge with brass headed tacks and finished with a bobble fringe.

The set of copper jelly moulds and four pewter dishes were displayed on the mantelpiece, together with Cook's tin tea caddy decorated with a coloured reproduction of Windsor Castle, a cocoa tin containing spills, various notes and scraps of paper stuck behind a stone jar full of spare buttons, hair pins, knobs off cupboard doors, pins, a reel of black cotton, a pair of scissors, a packet of pipe cleaners (though what Cook had these for is anyone's guess), various other small and potentially useful objects and a sprig of white heather sold to the superstitious inhabitant of the kitchen by a passing gypsy woman of good persuasive talents. Hanging on the wall above the mantelpiece was a solid, plain-faced kitchen clock with a loud and remorseless tick.

The centre of the room was occupied by a large deal kitchen table with two chairs tucked underneath while an old armchair reposed beside the stove, in a handy position so that those taking a rest could prop their feet up on the highly polished steel fender.

The floor was covered in brown linoleum which had seen much wear and better days, and there was a rag rug in front of the stove, on which, when he was out of favour in the front part of the house, Michael was wont to curl up and sleep.

Grannie visited the kitchen on a daily basis, at 10.45 each morning, to "give the orders". She carried a tiny wicker basket which contained all the necessities for her daily life, only using a handbag for shopping expeditions. This basket held her bunch of keys to unlock every conceivable piece of furniture, case or box, her reading spectacles in a case, a pencil, a small note book, a bottle of smelling salts, a tiny, laced edged handkerchief, a box of matches, a little silver penknife and a whistle for trying to get Michael to come back when he did not want to.

A chair had been placed ready for Grannie and she sat at the table, her little basket beside her, and put on her spectacles, while Cook unhooked the school slate that hung on a nail by the window, produced a slate pencil, and on this Grannie wrote in her delicate copperplate hand, after due consultation with Cook, the menu for the day's meals.

The food for use plus any "left overs" would already have been placed on the table for inspection, having been brought up beforehand from the larder in the cellar. These were duly inspected and apportioned. Then the store cupboard was unlocked and the copper scales used to weigh the ingredients for the day's dishes, as arranged and written on the slate.

Sugar, rice, flour, pulses, gelatine, spices, dried fruit, and much more was all neatly stacked on the shelves. No tinned goods were ever used in Grannie's kitchen, and packet stuff such as soups, gravies, custard or blancmange, out of the question!

Blancmange was made from cornflour, and cochineal was added if it had to be pink. Jellies were made from gelatine and flavoured with fruit from the garden, either fresh or bottled, and custard from milk and fresh, home produced eggs.

In the little red covered notebook Grannie wrote down which commodities were running short and needed to be re-ordered. Her task complete she retired to the drawing room to write letters and await the statuary beverage at precisely eleven o'clock.

This ritual was followed to the letter every day, unless something untoward occurred or was due to happen, except on Sunday, when meals for both days would be ordered on Saturday.

The only other times Grannie went to the kitchen (unless requested by the cook) were to interview the representatives from the various food shops in Reading who came for the weekly orders.

Not all food was brought to the door. Some arrived by post. Gramps had a regular order for kippers from the Isle of Man, smokies from Arbroath, bloaters from Yarmouth and flat fish from Dover, all of which were packed in "fish frails", flat bags of woven rushes, the contents wrapped in layers of waxed or greaseproof paper, the top of the frail sewn up with string and garnished with two labels.

One never comes across a frail these days, like the late lamented brown paper carrier they have been made obsolete by the ubiquitous plastic bag.

Everyone gathered in the kitchen each autumn for the ritual stirring of the Christmas puddings. Gramps came bearing a wine glass of brandy to add to the already rich mixture, while Grannie brought a number of the little silver threepenny bits, and we all stirred and wished and waited to see the cook fill up the bowls with the spicy mixture. It was, for a small girl, one of the highlights of the kitchen's year!

# CHAPTER TEN

# Of Maids and Men

Ladies, over tea in their drawing rooms in the 1920s and '30s, talked constantly of "the servant problem", and how difficult it was to get honest, hard working girls of respectable parentage, and how even more difficult it was becoming to keep them. There was always one, or more, of their "friends" willing to pay a pound or two over the odds for a well trained maid.

I remember my mother telling me, many years later, that Grannie's cook received about £35 to £40 a year, the parlour-maid £25 and the housemaid £20. When the latter two posts were combined, the wage was £30. The maids were supplied with two morning and two afternoon dresses, all their caps and aprons, laundry, bed and board and one afternoon off a week.

The first maids I remember were Nellie and Violet in the early and mid 1920s. Both were local girls and in a couple of years they were joined by Violet's younger brother, John, who came as garden and odd job boy when leaving school at 14.

Violet did not endear herself to anyone. In her mid-twenties she was sour-faced, uncompromising, and a grudgingly polite woman, but she was an excellent cook and stayed for quite some years before leaving quite suddenly. When I had "grown up" I was told that Violet had been seduced by the village rake, and left the district in disgrace!

Nellie was with us for years. She was a pretty, fair haired country girl with rosy cheeks and a ready smile. Often, when her morning's work was completed and luncheon over and all washed up and put away and the chenille cloth thrown over the kitchen table to indicate the rest period, and the maids had changed into their afternoon uniform, Nellie would take me for a walk in the fields. Sometimes when I was quite young, we would take my toys to the little tumble down rick in the hay meadow where she played wonderful games with me. It was a sad day for us all when Nellie got engaged to a boy from another village and later left to be married.

I do not remember who took Violet's place, but I vividly remember Smith who filled Nellie's shoes. A tall, angular, late middle-aged spinster, who had worked in the "best" houses and was always saying "her ladyship liked it done this way", or "her ladyship would not approve of that", which annoyed my usually calm grandmother intensely.

Smith (she insisted on being called Smith as she had been when in "her ladyship's" employ) would not accept the usual clothing supplied to our maids, but wore instead long skirted, black dresses down to her ankles, all enveloping aprons frilled down each side and caps with streamers fluttering to the waist that she had worn in her last position.

She did not like children and told Grannie she had been used to a nursery where nurse and nursery maids ruled the inhabitants, presumably with a rod of iron, and she did not like the fact that Miss Peggy, Masters Tom and Patrick, sometimes came into the kitchen. We took an instant dislike to Smith and must have made her life hell. Her departure, however, was entirely due to me.

Grannie, thinking it good for Smith to become better acquainted with her high spirited granddaughter, asked her to take me for a walk one afternoon. I demurred, and suggested instead a game in the garden.

I had guessed that Grannie would one day try and get co-operation from Smith in the matter of the young people, and I had long planned a move which I thought, rightly, would remove the obnoxious woman from our midst.

At that time I had just discovered the delicious concept of "Cowboys and Indians", and that afternoon I conned Smith into being a "beautiful Indian Princess", at which she was quite flattered and allowed me to stick a hen's feather in her cap.

However, this elevation to the royal house had disaster in store for the participant. I told her a posse of cowboys were on the trail of her tribe who had burned the white man's wagons and slaughtered their women and children. A lively pursuit ensued with me in a cowboy hat made of paper, astride a broom stick shouting "get up there" to this makeshift horse, which took place at the end of the vegetable garden well out of earshot and eyesight of anyone unless they had business down there. Unhappily for Smith they did not have any that particular afternoon.

Of course, after a chase, the princess was captured, and tied to one of the greengage trees by the length of rope I called my lasso. The wretched woman could not believe it when I wound the rope round and round her body and tied her securely to the tree trunk, and wailed mightily when I left her, telling her that no doubt one of her tribe would return and rescue her.

Well, the tribe proved very tardy, but an hour or so later John, coming into the garden after an afternoon hedging in the meadow, heard her wails and went to the rescue.

Tea was late and served by Cook, Smith was in her room packing her box, and I got severely ticked off and shut in our bedroom without tea or supper. Then there was the humiliation (which I richly deserved) of having to apologise to Smith before she left, which she did the next morning, riding into Reading on the carrier's cart, her box up behind.

The next two maids that come to mind are Alice and Sarah, two elderly sisters who lived in Zin Zan Street in Reading. They came with excellent references, albeit of a year or so back, but maids were getting hard to come by, so Grannie engaged Sarah as Cook and Alice as house parlour-maid, although my mother said Grannie had written to her and expressed her misgivings.

They were tiny and wizened, with grizzled hair, and they too wore long skirts with wrinkled, lisle stockings. We were not living at Foxhill then, but used to come for weekends, and I hardly ever went near the kitchen when Sarah was in charge as it smelt and she was fierce and did not suffer children gladly.

Alice one could not help liking, for she was a poor, apologetic creature, who worked hard but seldom made any impression on anything, and when empty handed always clasped her hands together holding them away from her body as if she were carrying some heavy burden. She was an avid bearer of bad news, ending her perorations with the words "Innernt it orful, M'um?" which saying was quickly adopted by the younger members and passed into family language; along with John's classic phrase, uttered in his broad Berkshire accent "Theys a frushie onner th' arge un 'e'ds puckin' er snoil!" Roughly translated, "There is a thrush under the hedge and he is pecking a snail".

Mother and I were living in furnished rooms on Caversham Heights and it was the end of spring term at school when we received an urgent telegram from Grannie which read, "Maids have left, can you come?" So we packed up everything, not an unusual occurrence in our lives, and went back to live for a time at Foxhill.

Things had got so bad that Grannie had been forced to tell Alice and Sarah that they had to clean up or leave. They had chosen to do the latter, packing their boxes that day and walking out without a bye your leave.

My mother's face when she saw the state of the kitchen was a picture. I was about thirteen at the time so willing and able to help.

The kitchen was indescribable. Every shelf was thick with black dust, the kitchener was encrusted with the residue from saucepans which had boiled over, soot and ash was piled everywhere in the grate.

The sink was black with grease, the kitchen table in the same state, we eventually took a knife to it and cut the grease off in strips.

The floor had not seen a mop in weeks. Stale and rotten food was discovered in the cupboards and the larder, the bread crock was half full of waste bread covered in green mould.

Saucepans were ingrained with grease inside and encrusted with burned food outside. The catalogue could continue.

Mother swathed us both in aprons and we set to work. It took three days to get rid of all accumulated grease and dirt, and give the kitchen any semblance of cleanliness. Then mother, whose talents were endless, set to and painted all the walls, ceiling, windows and doors before she was satisfied that the room was fit enough in which to prepare meals.

It seemed that Sarah had uttered an ultimatum to my grandmother: she was not to come near the kitchen, Sarah would go to her for the orders each morning and take the key and help herself to the dry goods. So at the mercy of her maids was she that Grannie had uncharacteristically given into pressure, but not for long. After a while she had gone to the kitchen, recognised the state of affairs, and ordered things to change, which they did not, so the whole thing ended with the departure of the old sisters back to Zin Zan Street.

Cleaning up the kitchen was bad enough, we then had to face the maids' bedroom, and I will draw a veil over the problems encountered, sufficient to say that both mother and myself performed the cleansing process with scarves tied round our noses and mouths!

We stayed at Foxhill that time for the best part of a year, and I went backwards and forwards by bus to school in Caversham.

It proved very difficult to get maids, as girls were by then finding more interesting and better paid jobs in offices and hairdressing, either of which were no doubt preferable to slaving over a hot stove or single handedly keeping a fairly large house clean and the occupants fed and happy for a minimum of pay and little free time.

However, after several false starts mother at last engaged a cook and a house parlour-maid for my grandparents, but the pair only lasted a week and then said they could not get on together and both threatened to leave.

The parlour-maid, in her early twenties, was a very fat, pink and white blonde girl with a happy smile. She came to my mother and said she was a good plain cook, and would be happy to stay and combine both jobs as she preferred to work alone. This pleased the cook as she wanted to leave anyway, so Florence commenced her twelve year reign which lasted until my grandmother died in 1946.

Florence was tremendous worker. She rose early, got the fire going, brought up the early tea, and had the rooms spic and span when the family came down to breakfast, which would be ready and welcoming on the table. She cooked and cleaned and scrubbed and polished, nursed the old people if they became ill, exercised Michael, coped with callers and visitors, and in short proved a valuable factotum for two elderly people.

Florence even found time to join me in acting out the plays I wrote. After dinner, when all was cleared up and put away, we would turn the kitchen into a "stage", dress up in old curtains and odd hats, and act out the rather lurid pieces I wrote. She also became an appreciative audience when I read out the poems I had written.

Florence was kind and cheerful, singing as she went about her work. She happily put up with "the Master's" eccentricities and occasional tantrums. She was devoted to Grannie and interested in all the family and friends who visited, remembering their likes and dislikes, from the second hot water bottle to an extra spoon for the Epsom Salts in the morning tea and the blackcurrant jam for breakfast.

If the maids came and went, the outdoor staff, both male, were more enduring. A permanent and endearing member of staff was Mr Slaughter, who came three days a week for all of my grandparents' years at Foxhill to pump out the sewage as he had done for other inhabitants before them.

Mr Slaughter was an old man but he never seemed to get any older. He had a jolly, ruddy weather-beaten face with twinkling blue eyes peering from a mass of laughter lines and shaded by huge shaggy brows. Stretching from ear to ear and framing his face was a luxuriant grey beard.

Mr Slaughter's outfit never changed, he wore a battered, greasy brown felt hat, a coarse grey shirt with a red and white spotted handkerchief knotted at the throat. A waistcoat made from mole skins was fastened by wooden buttons he had carved himself. A faded, fusty, tan corduroy jacket with huge sagging pockets, and baggy cord trousers tied under the knees with lengths of binder twine completed his attire while his feet were encased in heavy hob nailed boots.

The drains from the house ran into a tank set against Farmer Bunce's field at the rear of the property. A large iron handled pump stood over the tank, and Mr Slaughter worked this for over half an hour on each of his visits. The untreated contents of the tank were discharged into a ditch running along the hedge that divided the field from the vegetable garden.

In winter, when all the house windows were kept tightly closed, only those of us in the garden knew that Mr Slaughter was applying himself to his task, but in summer when he arrived and started pumping without alerting the kitchen first, the sound of the pump soon had the inhabitants scurrying round closing windows, for the effluvia sent out during this operation was something with which to be reckoned!

In late summer the field ditch sprouted with enormous tomato plants which grew from the seeds in the sewage in the rich soil. Gramps thought it a great joke and called them "Grannie's tomato plants", as my grandmother ate daily of the luscious red beauties brought in by Gramps from his greenhouse.

After his job was done Mr Slaughter came to the kitchen for a cup of tea and a slice of cake, and brought the gossip of the village. He also brought the smell of the sewage, but no-one minded, he was such a dear, wonderful old countryman, with such tales to tell of his days, firstly as a gamekeeper, then as a mole and rat catcher which job he combined with other menial tasks such as our sewage pumping.

John never thought of leaving, a tower of strength round the garden, with a tremendous respect for, and allegiance to Gramps, from whom he learned how to be a good enough gardener to get himself a secure place in later years.

The postman who ratatted the lion knocker around eight o'clock each weekday, and the paper boy whose cheerful whistle could be heard from some distance away, who delivered the *Daily Telegraph*, the *Express* and the *Financial Times*, and every week the *Radio Times*, came to the front door, only coming to the back door and into the kitchen at Christmas when Grannie came through to give them their Christmas boxes, and Cook gave them a warming drink.

Each week came the representatives from the Reading purveyors of fine food, to collect the orders. The man from Baylis the Grocers had been calling for years. He was a dapper little man in a bowler hat and with a respectful manner.

The man from the butchers, whose name escapes me, came on a different day and wore a straw boater, and the tall, rather lugubrious man with the drooping walrus moustaches and a cap came from Colebrooks the fish, fowl and game firm. Cook was empowered to make all these visitors a pot of tea.

Grannie dealt with them personally, handing them the carefully written list of requirements, enquiring about the price of coffee or lemon sole and whether the season's lamb was up to standard. She gave them payment for the previous week's orders, ensuring they receipted the bills, which she would file in a drawer in her desk in a very professional manner. No bill was ever left outstanding. "People should pay their way," she would say rather severely, "It does no-one any harm to wait for something until they can afford it." She abhorred the idea of hire purchase, considering it the end of civilisation!

All these men had called for years, and she knew all their names and how many children each had and was genuinely interested in their welfare and progress. At Christmas she was generous with gifts for the men and their families.

After the men for the orders came the delivery men. Colebrooks on Tuesday and Friday in a white van with green lettering, and the man from Baylis in a sedate brown van, the name of the store in gold on the side. After the delivery of grocery, Grannie would come along to the kitchen, unlock the store cupboard and see that all the new goods were safely inside before locking up again.

The most regular of the weekly callers were the carrier, the milkman and the baker, all part of the prolific Bunce family. The village would have been hard pressed to survive without the kindly and enterprising Bunce family.

The carrier, a Mrs Bunce, and her son came on Mondays, Wednesdays and Saturdays to collect the shopping list, the books to be changed at Boots Library and any prescriptions from the dispensary of that concern, returning in the evening with the order complete for a very modest charge. On Saturdays they ferried all the surplus produce from the various gardens in the village to the weekly market. It was a wonderful service for the country districts, and such enterprises flourished right up to the end of the 1930s.

The baker was the son of old Mrs Bunce who kept the village shop on the common, and he arrived each morning with a basket of freshly baked loaves, whose mouth-watering odour wafted through the house.

The milk came with Farmer Bunce, brother-in-law to the shop keeper. He was a red cheeked countryman in the traditional well worn, slightly greasy clothes over which he sported a khaki drill coat, and topped it off with a felt hat of dubious age. He drove a white painted float adorned with gold lettering and drawn by a sedate cob of advancing years.

The float contained a tall, ten gallon churn with brass fittings, and pails in the same fashion. The milk came to the house in an oval pail with a brass-hinged lid. Inside from a rail hung pint and half pint "dippers". Cook took her jugs to the door and the milk was carefully measured out. Mr Bunce also brought delicious cream and supplied eggs to the few in the village who did not keep a pen of fowls.

Mr Bunce called before breakfast and again before tea. Two milk deliveries a day before universal refrigeration was essential especially in hot weather. There was only one delivery on Sunday.

Saturday was pay day, and Mr Bunce was later with the morning delivery. Taking off his battered hat he would come into the kitchen to collect his payment and enjoy a cup of tea and, if he was late enough, Grannie would come through and they would have a chat about village affairs or his long and complicated family.

Mr Bunce had a small farm in the village where he kept a nondescript milking herd, a few pigs and a large number of fowls, ducks and geese. He owned the field behind Foxhill and turned his dry cows out there to graze before they calved. One spring there were four and I gave them names, Jersey, Jumper, Lilywhite and Daisy, and they became firm friends, coming when I called them to eat up any cabbage leaves I could sneak from the garden.

Jumper calved one night, and great was the joy when looking out of the bedroom window to see a small, red calf walking rather unsteadily beside the big cow as Mr Bunce drove them back to the farm.

Mr Bunce was also related to the ice cream lady, who bought milk from him to make the rich, yellow product that so delighted the children of the village, to say nothing of the adults.

Both milkman and baker were still driving their cobs up to the end of the 1930s but Mrs Bunce the carrier,

**101**

who for years conducted her business with the assistance of a sturdy mare and a covered wagon type of conveyance, at the end of the 1920s changed over to a motorised vehicle in the shape of a large and commodious van, much to the dismay of the older inhabitants, many of whom would not trust their precious orders or artefacts to the dubious assistance of this modern marvel! However, the carrier's new van appealed to the more progressive who thought it a great step up as orders could be collected and goods delivered in a much shorter time, in spite of the fact that the sedate pace of 25 mph attained by the van was hardly excessive! The arrival of the motorised vehicle gave the Bunce family another string to their bow, for they opened the village's first garage alongside their forge and wheelwright's shop.

# CHAPTER
# ELEVEN

# Happenings
# in the Cellar

The door from the hall led down a perilous flight of well-worn wooden stairs. Several people fell down them at different times, but the most spectacular fall was made by Florence going down with a large joint on a dish. She missed a step, lost her footing, landed on her ample backside and slid down to become jammed at the bottom.

Meat and shattered china littered the stone floor, and Florence, who fortunately was not hurt, got a fit of the giggles.

Grannie was expressing concern from the top of the stairs, while Gramps, John, Mother and myself had all rushed down the steps to the outside door to the cellar to get in and help, but what can you do with an eighteen stone girl wedged in a staircase and laughing helplessly, tears running down her face?

By this time Michael had joined in and was barking loudly from the top of the stairs and putting Grannie in imminent danger of following her maid to the bottom.

John went back up into the house and got behind Florence to give her a shove, and what with the laughter, Michael barking and a concerted cries of "PUSH!" it was bedlam. At the third attempt Florence suddenly shot out like a cork from a bottle, scattering us in all directions.

At the bottom of these suicidal stairs, the left archway led to the larder, dark and dank, stone flagged with one iron barred window above ground. A wide slate ledge, about four feet from the ground was situated along one wall.

It was a superb place to keep perishable foodstuffs as it was always cold, even in the hottest summers, although the maids said at such times the butter was not hard enough to pat up properly. (All butter sent to the table was patted up with "Scotch hands", two oblong, ridged, wooden paddles, which rolled the butter into neat tubes, or for parties could be made to fashion roses or swans should the operators be of an artistic turn of mind.)

If the butter did get soft in the cellar, Cook would wrap it in greaseproof paper, place it in a bucket, and lower it down the well to keep it at the right temperature. Milk and cream were often kept fresh in this way during heat waves.

The slate ledge groaned with joints and fowl, and game, left-overs, cooked vegetables, home made brawn, puddings and pies. Cook spent a lot of time traipsing up and down the cellar stairs to fetch food to be cooked, taking things down, besides bringing up a selection for Grannie's inspection each day.

In winter the larder got damp, and if the rain was heavy and continuous, the stone floor, which was several inches below the level of the rest of the cellars, would get covered with water, and Cook had to put on her rubber boots for her trips up and down.

Through the archway on the right hand side of the stair well was the front part of the cellar that faced south. Here were delightful scents, because small quantities of apples were stored on racks ready to hand when wanted for eating or putting into pies. Bunches of herbs hung from the beams as well as strings of onions.

There was a bench under the barred window that let the sunlight in, it looked out on the flowerbeds, and through a half broken pane came the scents, in summer, of the roses and Mrs Sinkins pinks.

A table under the window held the pots of geranium cuttings that would hopefully make more large plants to go in even larger pots to obscure the view from the dining room window, adding their own peculiar odour to the other scents.

At a bench set to one side, John cleaned the knives on a board using a coarse brown powder with its own peculiar but not unpleasant smell. The powder was sprinkled on the board and then each knife would be vigorously rubbed up and down and on both sides until it shone bright and clean, then it was polished with a soft cloth.

The newly burnished knives were supposed to be run through hot water before being used, but sometimes your food tasted suspiciously of knife powder so perhaps this little task was, in the hustle and bustle of the kitchen, forgotten, or maybe, more likely, the supply of hot water had run out!

Gramps used to take the opportunity of cleaning his clasp knives when John had finished his task. He had two, one an enormous affair, the blade of which folded into the carved horn handle when a spring in the back was pressed. He carried this in the pocket of his tweed jacket in winter and his knickerbocker pocket in summer, and, in consequence, wore holes in the lining of both, much to Grannie's annoyance who seemed to be constantly making new pocket linings.

Gramps also had a smaller knife that appeared when the two halves of the handle were drawn apart. These knives had belonged to his father and meant a lot to him. Today they are in my possession and still as greatly treasured.

In the season the cellar was used to hang game. Gramps liked his game high and he certainly saw to it that it was hung long enough! Pheasants and partridge are hung by the neck, and it was not until their legs assumed a greenish tinge and the skin of their necks began to disintegrate, that he considered them fit for the oven.

Gramps always plucked and cleaned the game himself, and absolutely forbade the cook to wash them out, a wipe with a dry cloth being all that was permitted.

Both mother and I abhorred high game and, in deference to our taste, which he could not understand in the slightest, Gramps always cut us slices off the breast of the birds, although this too, was tainted.

**106**

Rabbits were paunched and, like the hares, hung up by the back legs. The hares had a metal cup attached to their heads to catch the blood, which was used in the "jugging" process, jugged hare being one of the old man's favourite dishes.

Rabbits only hung a couple of days before being skinned and sent to the kitchen to be cooked, appearing cold in pies with slices of hard boiled egg all set in a delicious herb flavoured jelly, and topped by a golden crust. Sometimes the rabbit was served boiled with onion sauce, sometimes stuffed and roasted whole which mother disliked as she said they resembled cooked babies!

The frails in which the fish had arrived hung on nails round the walls and added to the mixture of smells. Sometimes a large ham hung from the beam, but if it got warm in the cellar it would be taken to hang in the larder.

Secured by a heavy padlock, a stout wooden door led into a small, low-ceilinged cellar where Gramps kept the wines, a few choice bottles for occasions such as Christmas or some family celebration, and his cider.

The cider arrived in a cask and was carefully transferred to the large bottles in which Grannie's Vichy water was bought. After filling each bottle, Gramps inserted four or five large raisins and put the corks in lightly, the theory being that after standing awhile with the raisins gently fermenting, a stronger and more palatable brew would result.

I used to thoroughly enjoy the bottling ceremony, helping him by the flickering light of a candle to stand

**107**

the bottles in neat rows on the long shelf in the cramped quarters of the "wine cellar", and inserting the raisins into the amber liquid and gently placing the corks in position.

One autumn something went wrong. Either he pressed the corks in too tightly, or maybe I did, but John reported to the cook, and the cook told the house parlourmaid who came in looking flustered at breakfast time and said, "Please, ma'am, but Cook says John thinks something has gone wrong in Master's cellar, 'cos there's a powerful smell and something's coming from under the door."

Something indeed had gone wrong, a dozen bottles had blown their corks, one at least had fallen over with the blast and brought down others, and there was cider running sweetly over both cellar floors.

Gramps thought it frightfully funny and roared with laughter, and said he should scoop it up and put it in a bucket for Cook to use next time she roasted a joint of pork! Michael sidled down and lapped up a good amount, and then went unsteadily up the stairs to the kitchen where he slept soundly the rest of the day!

It was under the shelf that held the cider that the Seakale was forced. The crowns were placed in boxes containing half earth and half compost, and then covered with old saucepans or buckets, and left to sprout. We had to keep a careful eye on them as earwigs love this sort of place to hide and breed, and would eat out the middle of the crowns, so an earwig hunt was regularly instituted.

When the crowns had sprouted, the boxes were dragged into the big cellar, but the covers kept on as Seakale is supposed to be blanched for use, and if uncovered when growing, turns green and is unpalatable. It is a most delicious vegetable, simmered until tender and served with a creamy sauce or melted butter. Strangely it does not seem to be popular these days, perhaps the growing of it, in modern parlance, is too labour intensive!

In the outer wall a door opened on to a flight of stone steps leading to the garden, and trained on the wall of the house was a Morello cherry tree, its branches spread wide and secured by a neat system of wires. This tree yielded large black fruits, too acid to be eaten raw, but making superb pies, jams and jelly. When the fruit was ripe we fought a losing battle with the blackbirds, who always managed to get their share of the fruit despite the whole tree being shrouded in netting.

On wet days Gramps and I spent a lot of time in the cellar engaged in all manner of jobs, like heeling Gramps's lace-up garden boots. He did this by placing the boot on a cast-iron "last" and expending much energy hammering on a new heel. Or we would prepare skins for drying.

All the rabbit skins, from his own Blue Beverans and those from wild rabbits, were scraped clean and then pegged inside-out on boards which Gramps had fashioned for this purpose, and then hung out in the air to dry.

Gramps also caught a lot of moles which were a pest in meadow and garden, their skins were also dried. Once he sent my mother a parcel of dried mole skins to make me a waistcoat. Mother put them away in a drawer and was a bit tardy getting on with the construction of the garment. Something must have gone wrong with the drying for, when she went to get them, she found the skins heaving with maggots! I never did get my much desired moleskin waistcoat.

Of course there were always cuttings to pot up, dried seed pods to be emptied put in envelopes and labelled, and in wet weather we plucked the fowls and game in the cellar. I was quite expert at this at a young age.

We also had a table for the egg racks in which all the home produced eggs were placed, some having to be washed and dried, and then sized, small for cooking, duck eggs for Gramps's breakfast and double yolks for me.

I was given a piece of flannel and encouraged to grow mustard and cress, and seed trays to germinate seeds for my own patch of garden and to grow acorns in pots.

The cellar was indeed, for me at least, a magical place.

# CHAPTER
# TWELVE

# From Back Porch to Garden

The back porch always smelt delightful, a combination of newly chopped wood, coal, boot polish, fresh vegetables, herbs and fruit. Each day in winter John brought in a box of wood chips for lighting the fires, a small basket of logs for the dining room, the anthracite hod for the drawing room stove, filled a brass coal scuttle for our bedroom and, all the year round, firing and two coal hods for the kitchen.

Every morning after replenishing the fuel stocks John's next task was to polish the shoes, although for some reason in winter Grannie preferred the boots to be cleaned in the cellar. The porch therefore had a slight whiff of Kiwi Boot Polish about it.

I remember my mother telling me that after service in the Boer War my father went sheep farming with a cousin in Australia and after a while travelled on to New Zealand. In New Zealand he met a man who had invented a new shoe polish. Daddy and the man became friendly, and my father was invited to join him in the manufacture and marketing of this new product.

Daddy, usually ready to take a chance, for some reason, saw no future in the plan and turned the offer down. The product was Kiwi.

Quite a lot of other things were kept in the porch, the housemaid's box, which was a square wooden bucket with handles, and contained compartments that held all the maid would need to clean grates, polish floors, burnish brass and wax the furniture, together with an assortment of brushes, dusters and cloths.

The maids' mackintoshes and rubber boots also lived in the porch, while the flue brushes hung behind the door together with the sink plunger and a coil of wire should anything stop up the house drains.

I used to like to sit on the porch steps in the sun watching the birds in the vegetable garden, getting ready to clap my hands when the blackbirds and thrushes invaded the strawberry patch.

Every morning Gramps would enquire of Grannie which fruit and vegetables were to be brought in, and one of his greatest pleasures was to dig the new potatoes, while he set me to picking peas or broad beans, or John to get up leeks and parsnips, depending on the season.

Lettuce, radish and spring onions were in abundance in late spring to be joined in summer by tomatoes and cucumbers from the greenhouse. There was always a plentiful supply of green vegetables, and rows of carrots, onions, turnips and swedes while the celery plants grew in a modest row with their paper collars round their necks to facilitate blanching.

One of Gramps's favourite vegetables was Kohl Rabi, a sort of green turnip affair that grew on a stalk above ground and was topped by a tuft of leaves. The leaves were served as a separate dish and were reasonably palatable, but the root I thought absolutely horrible.

Gramps also grew Salsify, which looks, when dug, like an anaemic parsnip. It exudes a powerful white juice which stains the fingers black of those who have to prepare it for cooking. It does however have a very unique and delicate taste, and was at its most palatable when it had been boiled until tender, rolled in egg and breadcrumbs and fried. It was often served in this manner as a savoury after dinner.

All the garden produce was trimmed and washed and sent in a basket to the back porch ready for cooking. This largesse was accompanied by herbs, parsley, sage and thyme, and as it sat in the porch awaiting Cook it gave off a lovely aroma.

A flourishing asparagus bed supplied the dining room with that luxury in season and the fern from the uncut stems provided backing in the vases for Grannie's floral decorations.

About 1932 Gramps added a mushroom frame, and great was the delight, after much trial and error, to see the white backs of the mushrooms pushing through the soil. This frame with its solid wooden top provided us with a splendid seat on which we could sit and discuss the affairs of the garden, and also watch the inevitable bonfire, both of us being addicts of burning up whatever waste we could gather.

The greenhouse, that never produced anything other than tomatoes and cucumbers, was watched over by an old and wise toad who had his home under the water tank. He had lived there years and was quite tame, coming out on occasions to blink at us with his amber eyes. Gramps used to catch the odd bluebottle and throw it to him, but he was never very grateful.

Strangely enough, Michael, who would kill anything that moved, never interfered with the old toad. When provoked toads exude a poisonous substance and this, if ingested, can prove fatal to dogs and cats. Did the wise old dog sense this?

There was a water tank outside the greenhouse where the produce was cleaned, and it also provided a "wash hands" place before we went in to lunch or tea, a rather raggety towel made from a cotton feed sack being kept in the greenhouse for us to dry on. Gramps considered this method of hygiene quite adequate!

The plans for the garden and the livestock were made in the study, but the day to day implementation of such was done in the shed.

The range of old wooden barns and stables backed on to Farmer Bunce's field. The first was the tool shed, where forks and spades, hoes and rakes, hung in shining rows, the second was Gramps's shed, full to the brim with everything needed for running a successful enterprise.

More prize cards the poultry and rabbits had won at shows were pinned on the peeling, whitewashed walls and liberally covered with dust and hung with cobwebs.

Saws and hammers and other tools were hung above the bench on which there were all manner of interesting objects, chief among them the oblong oil stone on which Gramps honed his knives.

The shed was redolent with the smell of onions, for they hung from the beams in ropes to dry while the shallots were spread in trays down one side.

Next to the shed was the old stable, still with the wooden pegs in the wall that had held collars for the work horses in days past. Here larger objects and feed for the livestock was stored, and mounting the ladder to the loft it was to find the rabbitry. Rows of neat hutches with their Blue Beveran occupants happily munching away at carrots, bran, hay and green leaves.

As the fruit and vegetables were picked or dug, they were transported to Gramps's shed for sorting and appraisal. Much of the fruit came into the house for consumption, bottling or jam and jelly making: apples, pears, plums, greengages, strawberries, loganberries, raspberries, gooseberries and three kinds of currants, and the inevitable rhubarb.

A thick row of Alpine strawberries, both red and white, bordered the whole length of the garden path, and when I had picked enough to fill a small bowl for Grannie, I was allowed to eat any left over. They were so sweet, and had quite a different taste to the strawberries from the big patch at the top of the garden.

The loganberries, some of the largest and juiciest I have ever eaten, grew on a trellis along the top of the compost pit, so when you were picking them you had to be very careful not to slip into its murky depths.

Anyone staying in soft fruit season was drafted into the garden to help with the harvest, as fruit that Grannie did not need for the house was packaged up and sent to market.

Down the side of one path grew the dessert gooseberries. One special bush was cultivated for Grannie and was called "Golden Globe". They were large and juicy, and my mouth would water just looking at them.

Of course it was forbidden to touch any of them, but occasionally I would sneak one from a lower branch at the back, and, well, they say stolen fruits taste the sweetest! However, I am sure Gramps counted the fruits everyday, because on the rare occasion when temptation got the better of discretion, he always knew and taxed me with it, and I had to own up and get a wigging.

Apple trees grew everywhere. Gramps was keen on Codlins, which are oval and yellow and I never thought very palatable. They also do not keep well, so quite a lot went to market, where others must have been of the same opinion as myself as the Codlins never fetched much money.

Gramps also had Bramleys for the apple pies, and Russets ready for Christmas, and several other old fashioned varieties. The apple picking was quite an event and lasted over a period of weeks, not all the varieties being ready at the same time.

Gramps and John clambered up ladders and leant on insecure looking boughs. Grannie would come out and stand under the tree often saying in a despairing tone, "Frank, I wish you would come down, you might fall." Of course he only chuckled and took no notice.

As the Codlins grew on smaller trees these were left to mother and myself and any visitors to gather. Uncle G and Aunt Mabel were great apple pickers and usually came to stay in September for the harvest.

I do not remember my cousins being a lot of help, Tom was always too tired and Paddy and myself when we got together were usually up to some mischief. One time we filled the garden syringe with whitewash and went round spraying it on the flowers and trees. The garden looked as if it had been invaded by giant birds, but the truth soon got out. Gramps saw the funny side of it; I'm not sure about our mothers and Grannie.

I had my own garden, a small triangular patch right at the end of the vegetable garden. It was given me when I was quite tiny and I was encouraged to grow anything I desired. Gramps was always giving me odd plants for which he had no further use or a left over seed potato. At one time my patch got quite overgrown with Lemon Balm which spreads like a weed. I also grew flowers from Bees Seeds then available for a penny a packet in Woolworth. Clarkia, Candytuft and Love-in-the Mist featured in no small measure, while Love-lies-Bleeding and Forget-me-Not came close.

I called my patch Paradise Garden, a bit of a misnomer as when we were not in residence it got quite overgrown and assumed the aspect of a small jungle.

**117**

My garden was also a place for picnics and celebration, and at the Silver Jubilee of King George V and Queen Mary, Paddy and I planted a bean stick with a Union Jack flying from it at the entrance. This was a signal for John to climb the Deodar on the front lawn and fly a similar flag from the topmost green finger.

Gramps was a great teacher and all his lessons were interesting and memorable, and my gardening lore, learned when I was small, has stood me in good stead through my life.

# CHAPTER
# THIRTEEN

# Grannie's Room

The long window at the head of the stairs gave a good view of the flower garden, and when open in summer the scents, and sounds of bird song, filled the passage to Grannie's bedroom. It was not a large room and appeared smaller than it was, being furnished in the solid Victorian style.

The large brass knobbed bedstead almost filled one wall with a bedside cabinet placed on either side.

There were two windows, the large one facing north and a small one in the west wall overlooking the long stretch of fruit and vegetable garden.

Grannie's dressing table was carved mahogany with three oval mirrors, and matched a massive chest of drawers and the wash stand with its rose covered china accoutrements.

Under the window was a padded stool, another of Michael's vantage points and one I often shared with him. It was off this stool and through this window that Michael, in his fifteenth year, made his spectacular descent to the flower bed below, emerging little the worse.

**119**

Grannie's room was a great place for confidences and secrets. She and mother used to shut themselves up for a good talk over some matter that neither Gramps nor I were supposed to know about. I loved going in when Grannie was dressing, especially when I was very young, to watch her put in the full set of dentures, although why this was so exciting I have no idea!

Mother often brushed Grannie's long black hair, only lightly streaked with grey despite her age, and dressed it up over pads made of real hair and fine wire, securing it by hair pins, kept neat by an almost invisible hair net.

A big cut glass bowl held powder with a fragrant scent which Grannie liberally dabbed all over her face with a large fluffy powder puff, and then wiped most of it off. This was her only concession to make-up in any form.

Grannie's jewel case stood on top of the chest of drawers, a large square box covered in green leather with a recessed brass handle and gilded trim to the edges. It was opened by inserting a curious round key in the lock, and twisting it in a special fashion.

It was a great treat when Grannie could be persuaded to open the box and tell stories of the treasures displayed in the three trays. There were her beautiful rings, the ruby and diamond, the five stone emerald and the gold band set with diamond chips.

Her engagement ring, one diamond and one ruby set either side of a pearl in a raised gold setting, she gave me on my eighteenth birthday, and a half-moon brooch set with the same stones to match on my twenty first.

**120**

The five stone diamond was the pick of the bunch and this my mother inherited only to sell it for a fraction of its worth to buy a Yorkshire Terrier show dog (her passion in life!) that never turned out as good as it was cracked up to be and eventually got sold on to America.

One of the favourite items in the jewel case was a solid gold mouse, his tail curled round the gold twig to which he clung while he feasted off a single pearl. This brooch was willed to my step-sister, but as she predeceased our grandmother it passed to Aunt Lovey and thence to her granddaughter so it, at least, is not lost to the family.

There were several lockets with little cut-out photos of relations on one side, and snippets of their hair on the other: Gramps at the time of his marriage and a curl of his Titian-locks, Great-grandfather, a patrician profile with his full bottomed white beard, a few strands of which were housed with his likeness, and Uncle G, a beatific child, framed with one of his dark curls.

When not in Grannie's little basket the gold lorgnette was kept with the other treasures. Sometimes I was allowed to press the hidden knob that shot these spectacles out of their gold handle and have fun peering at the other things through their powerful lenses.

One of Grannie's most exciting treasures, to all her grandchildren, was the tiny gold watch on its delicate chain that she wore secured to the bosom of her dress by a gold brooch in the shape of a bow. It had the most beautiful chimes and could be made to perform by pressing a little switch, and Grannie entertained all her grandchildren when tiny by making her watch "sing" at their request.

Another source of delight in this room were the pictures, all ninety-eight of them: mother and I counted them one day. Many were old photographs: my eccentric great-grandfather on his yacht, wearing his yachting cap with the peak over one ear, clad in a rumpled blazer and white trousers seemingly several sizes too large even for his ample frame. Another of him with a huge bell he had cast at the family works in South Wales, which was transported to his house at Brasted in Kent. He had it set up in the grounds and delighted in ringing it daily to the annoyance of all who lived in the vicinity.

There was a photograph of Grannie with the girls at her French convent, all in black, long skirted frocks, with hair severely dressed, and such serious little faces. "Why were you so sad, Grannie?" I asked once and she smiled gently and replied, "Well, we were all far from our homes and families and the convent routine was very strict."

Several faded photographs of Grannie with the grandparents who brought up her and her brother. Her grandfather was the famous civil engineer, soldier and explorer C. B. Vignoles, who as a baby had been lost for several years somewhere abroad after his parents died, and was only found by a cousin after much searching. Tales of this extraordinary relation kept me fascinated for hours.

122

The most exciting of these stories was that of his son Hutton, Grannie's father, who went with CB to Kiev to construct a dam over the Dnieper for the Czar. Hutton took his young wife and baby son with him, and my grandmother was born in Kiev. After the completion of the bridge the Czar presented the family with a snuff box set with precious stones. It would be interesting to discover what happened to this precious item.

There was a photograph of Cousin Lionel, an early and enthusiastic cyclist, depicted in tweed knickerbockers and jacket, with high, stiff collar and tightly knotted tie, a cap on back to front, posing with his machine. This, it was said, he rode very fast down the country lanes, swiping at the plants on the verges with a sword! Cousin Lionel had had a crush on my mother, and her brother and sister used to tease her unmercifully every time Lionel hove into view. "Laura, Laura, Lionel's come, put on your bonnet, my dear!" they would sing in unison. Not only did this irritate mother, but also the fact that they used her first name, Laura, which she hated, as it had been the name of Gramps's mother, her grandmother, and Aunt Laura the eldest daughter, both of whom she heartily disliked.

No, mother had a soft spot for Cousin Mervyn although he was several years her junior. A noted horseman, he had won the Military Cup for his prowess in the saddle on two occasions but was tragically killed in 1915 in the Great War. He too was up on the wall in Grannie's room, handsome in uniform and framed in filigree silver.

Cousin Amy peered from her wooden frame, pale and grim. It was said she had lost a foot in an accident and had a wooden one. I got told off for asking whether she unscrewed it when she went to bed.

There were several family wedding pictures but none of either of my mother's nuptials, both of which had been frowned on. On the other hand her sister's wedding was a very splendid and well documented affair, and strangely took place from my mother's house when she was still married to her first husband and lived, unhappily it was whispered, in some grandeur near Newbury. My step-sister, then three years old, was dressed fulsomely as was the fashion of the time, complete with huge hat tied with ribbons, and cajoled into carrying a basket of spring flowers. My mother used to laugh and tell the tale of how, in the middle of the ceremony, the bridesmaid's hat fell over her face and, as she tugged it off cried in a shrill voice, "Luddy hat!" Mother insisted the child had picked up the epithet from the servants! Wherever it came from it apparently convulsed the bride as well as many of the guests.

There was a very formal wedding pose of Uncle G and the formidable Aunt Mabel, the one looking impossibly sad and the other grandly triumphant in satin, Honiton lace and pearls.

I still have the picture of my mother, her brother and sister, taken when they were small children, Uncle G in a sailor suit and the girls in tailored dresses, Aunt with her roguish grin and my mother serious and rather sad-eyed.

The bedroom that my grandparents shared had a tranquil air, and smelt wonderfully of furniture wax, scented powder and lavender as there were so many home-made lavender bags in the drawers of the chest.

Once, however, this tranquillity was threatened. Gramps, who had many of his father's lovable but irritating eccentricities, decided to have his coffin made so that he could choose the one he liked with the right handles and made of oak that he had personally selected. He announced to Grannie that he intended to keep the coffin under the bed.

My grandmother put her slender foot down hard on this project, but he kept niggling on about it for some years, before finally giving in to his firm wife. Every so often however, he would bring the subject up again just to cause a little consternation which gave him a good chuckle.

On Gramps's side of the bed, a door led to his small dressing room. This too had one large and one small window so when he was dressing in the morning he could keep an eye on what was happening in his garden kingdom.

The room was furnished with a wash-stand with blue patterned china, and a tall chest of drawers on which stood a small wood framed mirror, his ivory backed hair brushes with his initials in silver on their backs, and a little pot of sweet-smelling pomade with which he dressed his flowing moustaches and little "goatee" beard.

A low table against the wall was covered in a cloth of red stuff, and held his Bible, prayer book and brass candlestick. Above it hung a crucifix and below was placed a kneeler. Every morning and evening Gramps said his prayers before this table, and his deep rumble could be heard by anyone passing the door at the time.

It was whispered in the family that Gramps, like several of his relations, had been a bit of a tearaway before he married, and then some years after his marriage and the arrival of his children, met up with a glamorous lady called the Countess Metaxa who got him hooked on religion, and proved quite a menace to the young married couple until my determined grandmother succeeded in ending the friendship. However, parts of the Countess's religious fervour clung to Gramps for all his life, and contrasted with his love of betting on horses and reading of murder mysteries, although his kindness of heart and spirit of generosity were never in doubt.

There were pictures in this room too, some religious, some photographs; the yacht again, this time with Gramps in a strange outfit, saw in hand, helping with a refit; one of Uncle G in uniform on horseback and a watercolour of a cock pheasant that I had laboriously painted for him one Christmas when I was twelve, which he prized as if it was an Academy accepted specimen!

The most interesting picture in this collection was of John Price, doctor to my grandparents and great-grandparents when they all lived in Wales. The picture showed a man with long, white hair and beard, clad in the robes of a Druid.

He had been a well known character of the time, and when not dressed as a Druid wore other strange garments including a cap made of a whole fox skin, the mask overshadowing his face and the brush hanging down his back. My mother told me tales of this strange man who she well remembered striding in at their front door and throwing his cap in a corner, and, as children, how terrified they were of him.

John Price had one son whom he christened Jesus Christ who died when a child. Price determined to cremate the body on a Welsh mountain top, which he duly did, despite the consternation and objections of local officials and general public. There were several pictures and a batch of clippings from the local press about this fascinating character and his strange doings, kept in Gramps's study. Some of these have survived the years.

Gramps kept his sporting guns, the old 12 bore known as "the blunderbuss", a 22 rifle for rook shooting and the "garden gun", an old 410 with which all the grandchildren were taught to shoot when they attained the age of seven years. Stored in their canvas covers in a corner behind the door, there were strict instructions that no-one, but no-one, was ever to touch them, and so far as I know, no-one disobeyed this order.

# CHAPTER
# FOURTEEN

# From Throne Room
# to Lounge

Between Grannie's room and the new wing was the bathroom which had been the boxroom and converted some time before by former occupants when the hip bath went out of fashion.

It was a small, narrow room with the long, deep bath taking up one side, and the lavatory of magnificent, mahogany proportions set on a raised step at the end facing the door; it earned this haven the nickname of the "throne room".

The bath was lined with something akin to papier mâché, indeed for all I know it could have been this substance, for it was rough and knobbly to sit on.

Water in the bath never exceeded a depth of more than three inches for the simple reason that the tanks were small and the kitchener was unable to heat more than this amount of water at any one time, and even then barely above the tepid. As the water was laden with iron, it came out of the tap bright ginger and the bath had a constant ring round it, which no amount of

Vim and elbow grease could shift. Those who bathed emerged with rust coloured feet and behinds.

Grannie had her "early tub" as she called it and then Mother and I shared a bath, she going first, so by the time I got in the water was cold. Gramps did not believe in "all that washing", declaring that it spoiled the natural oils of the skin and made one more liable to colds and chills. He refused to bath more than once a week, making his daily ablutions at the wash-stand in his dressing-room, taking his weekly bath before dinner each Friday evening.

For many years the maids did not use the bathroom at all, for their lavatory was an earth closet sited next to the coal shed at the end of the path that led from the back door. Presumably if they wanted a bath, they took it at home on their half day off on Sunday evening instead of attending Evensong. With the advent of Florence things changed a little, and she was permitted to have a bath on any weekday afternoon between two thirty and three o'clock.

When one was seated on the "throne", it was to look up and see over the door an ornate text, the words in heavy gold lettering. It read, "Beware, the Lord can see you".

This had a profound effect on me, I was worried that if He could see me then, I was not safe from his awesome gaze anywhere, for at that time the scriptures told (not as today) that God is a loving God so anything goes, but that if you did wrong God would see you and you would be adequately punished. The thought had a salutary effect on the behaviour of at

129

least one small child! There were only two pictures on the wall, one of Aunt Mabel in her wedding dress, which always raised a chuckle, not because of the subject which was pretty grim, but because my grandmother, who had a dry sense of humour, had caused it to be placed there.

The other picture was of great-grandfather's grave in Brasted churchyard, with its tall pointed monolith engraved with the names of his wife and all their children as well as his own. It was surrounded by heavy iron chains weighed down at the corners with enormous anchors, made in the family works in Wales and brought up to stand as a lasting memorial to him.

When the little church took a direct hit from a flying bomb in World War Two, this unusual memorial, standing quite close to the church door, was unscathed.

In later years, when I visited the grave for the first time, I remembered the text and thought no doubt the Lord could see him, probably standing right beside Him and instructing Him not to allow the enemy to destroy this earthly monument!

The maids' room, facing south with two windows, was situated off the landing, with pine furniture, and two single iron bedsteads, and curtains and wallpapers bright with little flowers. It was totally barred to all but the maids, as Grannie, was firm that everyone should have a place where they could be private and rest if they wished. In cases of illness the doctor entered accompanied by Grannie and my mother of course, who did any nursing required.

Through the door on the right of the bathroom was the "lounge". How this former bedroom, now a passage room to the new wing, came to be christened is a mystery. It was a very busy room and little time was available for lounging.

Firstly it held a gigantic mahogany "press" which filled the whole of the wall that divided the lounge from the bathroom. The highly polished doors of the top half of the press swung open to reveal shelves on which Grannie kept her clothes and some of Gramps's "best" shirts and other garments. The long drawers held the linen, while Grannie's dresses and coats hung in the wardrobe end.

Another shelf held all Grannie's hats, brown apart from the black felt kept for funerals. If all the hats were alike, the trimmings were different. Bunches of yellow flowers on one, birds' wings on another, one with a bunch of cherries.

Grannie had a rigid rule about wearing hats. No lady, she considered, would venture out unless wearing the appropriate headgear, whether for a walk in the lane, calling, shopping or church.

Indeed, so rigid was this hat-wearing rule that once, when my grandfather was in bed over a weekend suffering with a small complaint and he requested that the vicar come and give him Communion, Mother met Grannie on the landing that Sunday, wearing her best church-going hat. On enquiring why she was so attired, she was told that she was attending Communion in the bedroom, and when one did this it was customary to wear a hat. Mother protested that the bedroom was hardly consecrated ground, but my grandmother held staunchly to her views and wore her hat splendidly for the occasion.

Under the north window of the lounge stood a table, clad, as were so many others in the house, in the same nondescript red cloth. This held a lamp, the family Bible with all the births, deaths and marriages written in the front, and two huge brass bound albums of relatives past and present. The albums afforded my cousin Paddy and myself hours of pleasure and amusement on wet days.

Opposite the window was a large deal cupboard, once painted white but faded and well worn. The shelves contained all the bottled fruit, jams, jellies, marmalade, pickles and sauces made from the produce of the garden during the year. All the jars were neatly labelled by my grandmother, and arranged by year and in monthly order, so that the oldest would be used first. Possibly Grannie was one of the first to practise stock control!

Runner beans were dry salted and laid down in earthenware pots, while surplus eggs were preserved in Waterglass, in similar crocks. These containers were too large for the lounge and consigned to the cellar.

The lounge was also home to the laundry basket and hamper which would be filled with the soiled clothes and linen every Monday morning. This took place at the conclusion of my grandmother's upstairs visit at nine fifty, and before the flower ritual, and required not only my grandmother, but the maid and either mother or myself or both, although why so many souls were required to sort list and pack so little remains a mystery.

The laundry list was a long, slim blue covered book, and contained printed leaves listing the items in the basket, sheets, pillowcases, tablecloths, napkins, blouses, shirts etc. and at spring cleaning time, blankets and bed covers.

Mother attended to the listing until I was old enough to take over. Socks, stocking and woollen garments were washed by hand at home, all else was stowed in the hamper. When it was full the lid was latched with its metal fastener and made secure with a leather strap. John came to carry it down to the back porch, there to await collection.

The laundry man collected in the afternoon and left behind another hamper full of clean linen which we checked against another list the next morning.

In spite of all customers being given their own laundry mark which was inscribed in Indian ink on each item received, to say nothing of the fact that all Grannie's linen and garments were sewn with Cash's name tapes, things were continually getting lost, and there was a constant stream of terse notes sent to the laundry, demanding to know why there was a sheet or a shirt missing.

It was in the lounge that the luggage was assembled and packed for our grandparents annual holiday. John would bring down the big leather trunk and the dressing cases from the loft, and these together with Grannie's hat box, Gramps's carpet bag and a canvas hold-all for the rugs, walking sticks, fishing rods and umbrellas were all transported to Wales for just two weeks!

My mother used to protest at the amount taken, most of which was brought back unused, or indeed unpacked, but Grannie and Gramps were both adamant that each and every item might be needed should a given situation arise.

Gramps produced an amazing assortment of things to go in the trunk, including all he considered necessary should there be a train crash! Lint, iodine, bandages, salve and a dozen or more other medical items went in the trunk. The fact that it would be travelling in the guard's van and Gramps would be in the front of the train and therefore unable to get to it did not deter him in the slightest.

Grannie's hat box seemed to take not only hats, but every item that had been omitted from the main luggage. Mr Smith and John carried all this down to the taxi on the day of departure and allowed themselves a wry smile!

The lounge also acted as an overflow bedroom when the house was full of guests. There were only two spare rooms, the end one always being occupied by mother and myself, so if Aunt Lovey and my two cousins came, she had the other spare room and the boys slept on camp beds in the lounge.

Usually they brought their own beds, but once arrived with only one. From some dusty recess in the barn Gramps triumphantly produced the camp bed he had used when in the Militia in Wales in the 1880s.

Once the dust and grime had been removed it looked fairly sound for such a relic of the past, with only a trace of rust on the hinges and woodworm in the legs. Paddy volunteered to sleep on it. The camp beds were placed side by side with their heads to the little blackleaded grate, and we all trooped in to see the occupants safely installed.

Halfway through the night there was a crash and a yell and when we crowded in with our lighted candles, it was to find the front end of the antique bed had collapsed and Paddy had shot head first up the chimney! We all found this immensely funny, even the victim, once rescued from his predicament, joining in the laughter.

Gramps, of course, would not admit there was anything wrong with his camp bed, simply saying "that boy had not put it together correctly". He later proceeded to lend it to someone else who stayed and the same thing happened, only that victim was not nearly so amused. Grannie forbade the use of it ever again, much to Gramps's chagrin, who took to assembling it in his shed and using it as a seat.

Three steps down from the lounge and there was the bookcase. To me this was a treasure house. Here I found all the Tarzan books which are a wonderful read, and so unlike the distortions of the cinema versions of these tales, almost unrecognisable on screen.

Here too I found "*The Scarlet Pimpernel*" and other Baroness Orczy books in which I revelled.

I agonised over the heroine of "*Esperance*", the story of a love lorn Victorian maiden all muslin and camellias, who faded away for love of the dashing and handsome Claude Magnay, who apparently was too much of a wimp to ask her to marry him and put her out of her misery.

Chief treasure was that marvellous Australian story "*Robbery Under Arms*" by Ralph Boldrewood, which I read so many times I almost knew it by heart. I thrilled to the tale of Captain Starlight and his wonderful horse Rainbow, the weak willed Dick and his unfortunate family, honest brother Jim, sister Aileen, the old Irish mother, and Maddy who loved them all. (Another book utterly ruined when it was filmed.)

Of course there were books I was told were for grown-ups only. One was a copy of Ouida's "*Moths*", although, looking back (after I realised the subject matter), I cannot think how it got on Grannie's bookshelves, unless left by a visitor. Certainly Grannie never read it and if she had, would not have understood a word!

There were several Ethel M. Dell and Ruby M. Ayres novels, favourites of my mother, and a worn set of "*The Queens of England*", which I found interesting as I got older.

I can so well remember on wet days, sitting on the steps and being so absorbed in a book that I did not notice how dim it was getting or how the time had passed.

# CHAPTER
# FIFTEEN

# Along the Passage

There was a north window in the passage and this faced the door into the smaller of the two spare rooms. When I was a little girl I was allowed to use this as a play room, and here I kept my collection of teddies and stuffed toys; I hated dolls of any kind. I also had a farmyard with a farmhouse and lead animals, a pond made from mother's handbag mirror and bundles of hay and straw bound up for me by Gramps.

From early childhood, and as soon as I had leaned my letters, I started writing. Mother, who had no bent for this and who only grudgingly attended to her correspondence, could not understand my delight in scribbling away for hours, and was all for me finding something more worthwhile to employ my time. I was, however, never deterred and wrote little stories and poems as well as plays for my toy animals to perform.

The single bed would be pulled away from the wall, and I knelt behind, making my toys act out the parts as I spoke the lines and sang the songs I had composed.

Such an enterprise requires an audience, so Grannie and mother and anyone visiting were invited to attend the performance, being supplied with bedroom chairs at the cost of one penny each, the proceeds being sent to Dr Barnardo's.

I adopted this charity at an early age when they sent round collecting cards painted with little coloured balloons in which donors inscribed their names. It was a good ploy, and caught my imagination, and the audience for the plays were helpful in filling up the balloons.

It was in the spare room that the Dog Club was born. I was about nine or ten and of course we always had dogs as mother had bred and exhibited Yorkshire Terriers since 1906. Then there was Michael and all Grannie's friends and our relations had dogs. All owners approached joined the Dog Club, which cost one penny, and each member was supplied with a monthly magazine. This consisted of little sheets of paper sewn together with coloured wool, and written and illustrated by myself.

I made around a dozen copies before enthusiasm ran out and then advised members who did not have a copy, to borrow one from their friends! I cannot remember what I wrote for this first essay into publication, but I am sure many of the recipients had a good chuckle.

One spring I ran a flower show for the Dog Club and members were invited to send in a flower arrangement. Strangely a number of people did just that. My mother was the judge and all unwittingly chose an arrangement of bluebells and fern, only to find it was my entry, put in for Michael!

When Uncle G and Aunt Mabel stayed, the spare room seemed to be filled with sensible shoes and bottles of cure-alls. Aunt Mabel was a great believer in Epsom Salts, and when the early tea came up, that extra teaspoon had to be placed on her tray, and she measured out the nauseous medication for her long suffering husband as well as herself, tipping it, not into a little water to be swallowed at a gulp, but in their first cups of tea. My mother used to shudder at the thought, and strongly resisted all Aunt M's attempts to get her to take this concoction for the rheumatism from which she suffered. The cure, said my mother, would be worse than the disease.

When Aunt Lovey stayed, the spare room was full of the scent of perfume, sheer silk stockings dangled from chairs, fashionable dresses hung in the wardrobe and dainty, high heeled pumps stood in a neat row under the dressing table.

Aunt L was only a tiny four foot eleven inches with size two shoes. She lived in London where she and her sons had moved from the Derbyshire estate she had shared with her, by then, estranged husband, and led a busy social life. I loved to watch her make up, she had a pretty, pert face with a real Cupid's bow mouth and used lots of lipstick, and her big eyes were fringed with long lashes that she stiffened and curled with mascara. She painted her pointed nails scarlet as was the fashion of the day.

Aunt L used to let me go in her room and put on lipstick, but I had to clean it all off before I went downstairs.

Gramps hated make-up and used to snort, "Really Lovey, I cannot think why you want to put that stuff on your face, and it looks as if you have dipped your fingers in blood!" But Aunt L just laughed and planted a kiss on his cheek leaving a lipstick smear, which he scrubbed off with his handkerchief. But his eyes were twinkling, he would forgive his beloved younger daughter anything.

It was always fun when Aunt Lovey and the boys came, she was so full of life and made everything amusing and was noted for starting wild schemes of one sort or another.

Once she and the boys decided to breed cage birds, turning a room in their flat into a bird room with cages all round the walls. They did well, even branching out to the showing world, and won a number of prizes. However, cage birds spill seed, and mice love seed, and in less than no time the block of flats in Chelsea where Aunt L lived had a plague of mice all beating a path to her door, and the bird breeding came to an abrupt end.

After that they took up tropical fish and filled the room with tanks, but a disaster with the water supply ended in the flat below getting flooded in the dead of night, and the fish plan was hastily aborted.

After that they acquired "The Pig", which was a small, hideous amphibian, lizard type creature who lived in the wash bowl in the bathroom. If you wanted to use the bowl you had to transfer The Pig to the bath. However, The Pig grew at a rapid rate and got so big he had to live in the bath, so when anyone wanted to bathe, The Pig had to be put on the floor, but not for too long as he required to keep his feet in water, so bath times had to be very hurried.

Eventually The Pig got so big he had to be given to London Zoo, much to the grief of the three inhabitants of the flat, but to the relief of visitors who, after his departure only had to run the gamut of the parrot, the assorted Cocker spaniels with smelly ears, the Pekinese with guarding tendencies, the French Bulldog with flatulence and the tom cat, who, if not carefully watched, piddled up their legs.

The big square bedroom at the end of the passage was always known as "our" room, and although other members of the family slept there on visits to Foxhill, Mother and I were its principle occupants.

It was furnished like the others, the inevitable bedroom suite complete with wash-stand and patterned china. Another double bedstead with brass ends housed a feather bed on top of a horsehair mattress. No pulling up the bedclothes in the morning, all beds had to be flung open to air and the feather bed pummelled to get all the lumps out of it before the bed was made up.

The stiff linen sheets were edged with crochet lace made by Grannie. My favourite edging was the one with teddy bears in the pattern and there was one with swallows in flight and another of roses.

The linen sheets were terribly cold in winter and even the two hot water bottles, a rubber one for your back and a stone one in a woollen jacket for your feet, failed to warm all parts of the bed, and one lay shivering until the bottles and the featherbed created a satisfying pool of warmth. In summer the featherbed was stifling hot, but even in a heatwave was never removed.

There were two photographs on the walls, both of Gramps's brothers. Great Uncle Tudor, handsome and erect, a pillar of Glamorganshire society where he had been a magistrate and also a well known horseman and supporter of the Hunt, and Great Uncle Barry, mother's favourite uncle, who was one of the first gentlemen in England to own a motorcar. A handsome man with sweeping moustaches, photographed in an astrakhan collared coat with one of the orchids he was famous for breeding in his buttonhole. Mother used to tell me stories of how Uncle Barry used to take her to the "motor racing" at Brooklands.

The rest of the pictures had been painted by my mother when she was a child. She became a not inconsiderable artist. Two landscapes on one wall and beside the bed an oblong picture of a stream with rushes growing and pink water lilies, painted when she was eleven. Over the bed hung a picture entitled "The little crossing sweeper", a haunting portrait of a boy in drab, late Victorian clothes leaning on his broom in an attitude of exhaustion. His thin, white face with dark circles under the eyes stared out at me in the candle light on winter nights, and I often thought of mother's story of how, when she was allowed to sketch him, he was suffering from consumption and died soon after the painting was finished.

Two windows in the room faced north and south and one summer night a bat flew in the south window, doing several laps of the room before falling in and out of the water jug and departing via the north window. My mother missed most of the fun for as soon as the bat swooped in, she shoved her head under the pillow, being convinced that all bats were looking for a lady's head of hair in which to burrow.

Another missile that came through the south window, only during the daytime, was a large sliver of wood that buried itself in the ceiling and left an indelible mark. Gramps had a great idea of blowing up tree stumps with dynamite. One however was a bit too explosive and the chunk in our ceiling was just one of the consequences; after that Grannie stopped this little excitement.

We were frequently roused quite early in the morning by the heavy pounding of footsteps along the passage, the door would burst open, and Gramps, roped into his blue, wool dressing-gown, a red "fez" on his head (he had acquired this in Algeria on his honeymoon) and carrying his 12 bore, would rush to the window, throw it up, and blast away at the rabbits that invaded the lawn as the sun rose.

Some years later when I saw the play "The Chiltern Hundreds" and the main character behaved in similar fashion, I supposed that all eccentric old country gentlemen went on like this!

Mother hated loud bangs and at the sound of her father's approach once more buried her head under the pillow, only coming out when assured the fusillade was over; Gramps used to laugh hugely at this performance and stump off to get dressed.

He would quite likely appear again before we were up. Carrying his tweed cap carefully against his chest, he would unfold it and roll a surprised hedgehog on the bed.

Morning tea was brought by the maid at seven thirty. The tea set was small and fine and painted with teddy bears. It was accompanied by a plate holding the thinnest slices of bread and butter.

Our room had three outside walls and in winter could be incredibly cold. When we came up to wash before dinner in winter, it was to find a lovely fire burning and there were glowing coals and bright flames to warm us. In very cold weather the fire was laid and lit before we rose in the morning, so we could dress in comfort. How pampered and lucky we were.

Mother and I always enjoyed this spoiling, for our life away from Foxhill was quite spartan. Money was always a problem after the death of my father, almost at times non-existent, and mother kept us by using her many talents for painting, sewing and cooking. I am sure our visits to Foxhill came as a welcome relief to her from all the work and worry and shortage of provisions she endured.

Looking back, I am convinced, that although I never wanted for food, she often had too little, making the excuse that she "was not a big eater". This was given the lie when we were at Grannie's, for mother ate well at every meal. However, somehow she managed for many difficult years, always keeping up appearances and never letting go for one minute.

When my mother went down with rheumatic fever one January, she lay swathed in cottonwool in the big brass bedstead. Here we all came to sit and cheer her up, taking her little dogs for walks, bringing her the first spring flowers, and often a baby rabbit or chick to stroke.

Mother was a great favourite with all the maids we ever had, and Cook made tempting dishes for the poor invalid, carrying them up herself to make sure they were consumed, as they would do the sufferer good.

Dr Hill, the good looking doctor with the perfect bedside manner, came daily from his surgery in a nearby village, stayed to chat and reassure mother that he would get her up and about as soon as was possible. Various friends and relatives called and tut-tutted while leaning on the bed end, at the sight of such a vibrant, energetic person laid low.

However, mother gradually recovered, and with Dr Hill's help and the love and care of the family and the maids, she was at last downstairs and convalescent.

I have vivid memories of lying ill in bed in this room. As we had moved about so much my schooling had been very fragmented, but from just before my twelfth birthday I had been settled at the Caversham school. As I took extra elocution lessons and had done quite well in the London Academy of Music elocution exams, I was cast as Titania in the fairy scenes from "A Midsummer's Night's Dream" to be performed as part of the end-of-term concert just before Christmas.

My joy at the casting was short lived, as those who had been pupils at the school since Kindergarten days,

**145**

remembered a previous production of these scenes, when "Bunny", the much worshipped Head Girl and Games Captain, had taken the part with conspicuous success.

I had never met this wonderful girl, who had, at fourteen, gone on to a grander school, but I was determined to give such a performance in my leading role, that I too, would be remembered long after I left, and secretly I hoped my performance would eclipse that of the famous Bunny.

I was word perfect long before the other members of the cast, and at the end of a cold day in the hall for the dress rehearsal, clad in a pale blue muslin gown made by my mother land wearing a star-spangled crown on my long hair, I actually received a splatter of applause from the staff seated in front.

It was as well I had this little moment of glory, for I caught a severe chill that day, and spent the night tossing and turning, and woke with a high temperature. When I got out of bed my legs buckled under me.

Doctor Hill came, prescribed and sympathised, and mother used the hallowed telephone to inform the school that I was ill and unable to take part, and she hoped they could find a replacement at such a late hour.

I lay burning hot with fever, cuddled up in the featherbed under the eiderdown patterned with Chinese dragons, birds and flowers, feeling so ill and crying miserably.

After a while the dogs came and jumped up on the bed, offering their unconditional support and sympathy

**146**

as only dogs can, and a stack of books and Dr Hill's visits resigned me to my fate.

I was well enough to attend the last day of term and went to collect my things. The girls, even the ones I thought were my friends, said in loud voices what a coward I was, how the story of an illness was made up, and how I had got cold feet as I knew I could not be as good as Bunny in the part. It was all so unfair, and when I heard that Bunny had been sent for to replace me and had played the part with the book in her hand to a standing ovation, my bitter cup overflowed.

I gathered up my things and left with out saying goodbye to anyone. I was just fourteen and never went to school again.

However, the old bedroom held more happy memories than sad ones. Waking up on my birthday to find a pile of presents by the bed, or at Christmas, when a bulging pillowcase would be suspended from the bed post. Lying sleepily watching the frost patterns on the window melt as the little fire caught alight and the flames danced up the chimney, or just waking to bright spring or summer sunshine, to know there was another day to be enjoyed at Foxhill.

# CHAPTER
# SIXTEEN

# Easter at Foxhill

Easter and Foxhill are inextricably entwined in my memories of the old house. We always seemed to be there at Easter and the sun seems to have shone all the time and there were primroses and daffodils in profusion.

A walk to the lovely woods a mile or so up the road, was to find primroses growing in a thick yellow carpet and I would pick quantities of the sweet smelling blossoms, tying them into small bunches with wool from the ball I had carried in my pocket for just such a purpose. I secured the bunches to a wand cut from a bush and, hoisting it over my shoulder, marched back to Foxhill, singing or whistling all the way from sheer joy of living.

It was required that when staying at Foxhill, I attended church with my grandparents. Mother seldom came, indeed when we were not at Foxhill neither of us went to church, but my grandparents played by the rules. I cannot say I was an enthusiastic churchgoer, as the curate, Mr Gwatkin, used to preach boring sermons that could last nearly an hour.

I tried several tricks to get out of going on various occasions, like getting myself covered in earth or coal dust, a pretty pathetic ploy as I was soon forced to change and wash. Once I staged a dramatic fall down the drawing room steps and feigned a sprained ankle, but although my grandmother was taken in, there was no fooling my mother!

The whole paraphernalia of Easter started on Shrove Tuesday when Cook made pancakes and the whole family trooped to the kitchen to toss them, even Grannie, who was not very expert.

After that Gramps went on a Lenten fast, not eating any meat or smoking his pipe for six days of the week. Apparently Sunday did not count, because he always made a good meal off whatever beast was roasted and brought to the table, and puffed away contentedly on his pipe the whole of the day.

Good Friday started early. Gramps did not break his fast at all and walked the mile to the Mission Church for Communion, walked home, and then set off again to attend the three hour service which started at eleven. Grannie joined him for the last hour, conveyed to the church in Mr Smith's taxi. It was one service I was, thankfully, not expected to attend.

The old people arrived home around two thirty, my grandfather in a state of exhaustion. He kept this up into his late eighties, when Doctor Hill forbade him to go without food for so long.

The Good Friday meal served at three o'clock, consisted of dried salt fish which had been steamed or boiled. I thought it was without doubt, the most disgusting thing to have to eat, especially when served with plain boiled potatoes and greens! Teatime brought a large plate of hot cross buns which helped to drown the memories of salt cod!

Easter Sunday remains a wonderful memory. There were gaily wrapped boxes of chocolate eggs for me, and the boiled eggs served at breakfast were all dyed different colours.

We dressed carefully for church, even my mother coming along sometimes, and any other relatives who happened to be staying.

The service was uplifting, with the familiar Easter hymns and everyone singing lustily. If the sermon was a bit long winded, I had fun watching the choirboys fidgeting and trying to crack nuts or eat sweets without anyone hearing or seeing them.

Then there was the amusement of watching the early spring fly that came to circle round my grandfather's bald head, and to watch him covertly slapping at it as it made a tentative landing on his shiny, pink scalp.

Back out in the sunshine, the younger members walked home down past Miss Vyner's cottage and into the Stile Field, where the first wild flowers were starting to bloom, while the older members of the party were driven home in Mr Smith's taxi.

Served at one o'clock, Easter Sunday dinner was traditional, a leg of prime Welsh lamb sent up specially from the Principality.

It was served with mint sauce and garden vegetables, and followed by a pie containing (what else?) the early forced rhubarb.

Sometimes Mr Gwatkin was entertained to this meal. In fact he ate quite a few meals at Foxhill. He was a tall, lugubrious man who cycled out from his home in Caversham every Sunday all through the year, to take three services and Sunday school at the Mission church, the Vicar hardly ever venturing up from the main church in the village at the foot of the hill.

Rumour had it that Mr Gwatkin and his wife had a large number of children, some said twelve, and that the family were very hard up. Judging by his under-fed appearance (he was painfully thin) and his frayed collars and cuffs, the rumour were probably true.

The Curate had to be entertained every Sunday by someone, parishioners taking it in turn to provide either breakfast after Holy Communion, Sunday dinner after Matins, tea after Sunday school, and supper before Evensong, after which he mounted his bicycle and rode the eleven miles home.

Everyone groaned when it was known Mr Gwatkin was to come for a meal. He was so sad and so boring, rather like his sermons. He was a prodigious eater, consuming everything put before him and always accepting second helpings, so that all agreed that Sunday was possibly the only day when the poor man got properly fed. This helped everyone's feelings of Christian goodwill, and made the two hours of his visit bearable to some extent.

There was a spring when my grandfather thought they should sell Foxhill and move to a smaller house with less land. Children were not told what their elders and betters had in mind, so the first thing I knew about the plan was when two men arrived with a huge FOR SALE sign and nailed it on two stout posts at the back gates.

I was so devastated at the idea of the only safe and stable place I knew being sold that I rushed indoors weeping as the men finished their task. 'Why, why?' I wanted to know, we were all so happy. All I was told was that it was no business of little girls. I fretted for days, vowing to myself that when I was grown up I would return and buy Foxhill myself and keep it just as it was, forever.

However, I need not have worried, although the asking price (I learned in later years) was only £1000, no-one, as far as I know, came to view, or if they did, they failed to make an offer. The board got old and weathered and eventually fell off the posts and the lilac bushes covered it discreetly with their green branches.

As I grew into my teens, Foxhill provided new and interesting amusements. I had by then started to wear pretty dresses, my long hair had been cut and was properly dressed, and by the time I was sixteen I was allowed to wear discreet make-up.

I went down to stay with Grannie and Gramps on my own one Easter, and the inevitable church visit was paid on Easter Sunday. Gramps informed me that Mr Gwatkin had been moved to another parish, as a vicar this time, and a Mr Salt had taken his place. Mr Salt was quite young and lodged in the village.

Our pew in the church was one from the front, and there I was in quite a stylish dress and a little hat, with just a touch of lipstick and mascara, much to Gramps's disgust! And there was Mr Salt all clean and scrubbed, with his fair hair sticking up in whisps, and clad in a pristine white surplice minus the creases that had characterised Mr Gwatkin's appearance.

I fastened my eyes on him, allowing what I fondly believed to be a coquettish smile to play around my lips, and was enchanted when he turned bright red and forgot his lines. All the time during the service, except when heads were bowed in prayer, I kept an eye on him and he on me.

The following day at tea time, Florence came in with "Please, M'am, the Curate has called". And there was Mr Salt, pink and white as a sugar mouse, and all flustered, and did hope it was not inconvenient, but was in the vicinity and thought he would call about the Lesson for next Sunday.

The next day I left to return home. Grannie wrote that Mr Salt had turned up on the Friday as well, but finding the bird had flown, did not stay for tea. "I think he is perhaps a little taken with you," she said in her letter.

It was at Easter when I was nineteen that my grandfather, then in his 93rd year, complained of feeling very tired, took to his bed and died quite quickly and peacefully, the great heart that had served him for so long and so well at last worn out.

I did not go to his funeral, it was as if I could not accept that the great character who had been so much part of my childhood, and around whom so much fun and happiness was woven, would ever die. So I stayed at home.

The funeral was attended by a large number of relatives and friends and, as with most of our family gatherings, did not pass off without incident. Mother and Aunt Lovey had an altercation in the churchyard with Aunt Lily who wanted to be the one to support Grannie, and apparently a great deal of jostling took place, with the ladies treading on each other's feet. How Gramps would have chuckled!

A few months later I went down to stay with Grannie, who seemed to be the only one who understood my absence at the funeral and, as we stood in a shaft of sunlight in the quiet drawing room she said, "I can still feel him everywhere, can you?"

Foxhill was too large for Grannie on her own, so she went to live in a small house in the country a few miles from Weymouth, to be near Uncle G and Aunt Mabel.

There was an auction of the surplus furniture and belongings that would not fit into Grannie's new home. I did not go, I could not bear to watch things I had grown up with and loved so dearly pawed over by strangers. And then finally, the house itself was sold. It was the end of my childhood.

# A Watching Brief

It is now 60 years since Foxhill was sold. Over those years my cousins and I have all visited the village at different times to find out just how the old house fared in modern times.

An early buyer cut down the Deodar and the Monkey Puzzle, and painted an enormous parrot on the end of the house. The next owners dispensed with the parrot and either they, or the following people, sold the meadow which was quickly built on.

The house looks much the same except that an extra piece has been built on the end of the study, it is rather well blended with the original. I do not know how the back of the house has fared.

At some time the vegetable garden was sold and two houses now stand on it, only a small portion of the once giant laurel hedge is still growing.

The recreation field behind Miss Ludlam's house was sold to build a housing estate and Farmer Bunce's land behind Foxhill is now the recreation field. There are houses built on both sides of our lane, now a road with a new name, and the Stile Field is a road with houses both sides. Much of the common beyond Foxhill appears to have been built over, but such are the changes that it is difficult to recognise much of the area. The road to Reading is now wide and busy, and whereas the old Three Firs public house, a wonderful black and white 16th century inn, was demolished years ago to make way for road building, the red brick bulk of the Rising Sun still stands where it always stood, a signal to the road that led to Foxhill.

**ISIS** publish a wide range of books in large print, from fiction to biography. Any suggestions for books you would like to see in large print or audio are always welcome. Please send to the Editorial department at:

**ISIS Publishing Ltd.**
7 Centremead
Osney Mead
Oxford OX2 0ES
(01865) 250 333

A full list of titles is available free of charge from:
**Ulverscroft large print books**

**(UK)**
The Green
Bradgate Road, Anstey
Leicester LE7 7FU
Tel: (0116) 236 4325

**(Australia)**
P.O Box 953
Crows Nest
NSW 1585
Tel: (02) 9436 2622

**(USA)**
1881 Ridge Road
P.O Box 1230, West Seneca,
N.Y. 14224-1230
Tel: (716) 674 4270

**(Canada)**
P.O Box 80038
Burlington
Ontario L7L 6B1
Tel: (905) 637 8734

**(New Zealand)**
P.O Box 456
Feilding
Tel: (06) 323 6828

Details of **ISIS** complete and unabridged audio books are also available from these offices. Alternatively, contact your local library for details of their collection of **ISIS** large print and unabridged audio books.